impact

3B

SERIES EDITORS
JoAnn (Jodi) Crandall
Joan Kang Shin

AUTHOR
Diane Pinkley

NATIONAL
GEOGRAPHIC
LEARNING

CENGAGE
Learning·

Australia • Brazil • Mexico • Singapore • United Kingdom • United States

Thank you to the educators who provided invaluable feedback during the development of *Impact*:

EXPERT PANEL

Márcia Ferreira, Academic Coordinator, CCBEU, Franca, Brazil

Jianwei Song, Vice-general Manager, Ensure International Education, Harbin, China

María Eugenia Flores, Academic Director, and **Liana Rojas-Binda**, Head of Recruitment & Training, Centro Cultural Costarricense-Norteamericano, San José, Costa Rica

Liani Setiawati, M.Pd., SMPK 1 BPK PENABUR Bandung, Bandung, Indonesia

Micaela Fernandes, Head of Research and Development Committee and Assessment Committee, Pui Ching Middle School, Macau

Héctor Sánchez Lozano, Academic Director, and **Carolina Tripodi**, Head of the Juniors Program, Proulex, Guadalajara, Mexico

Rosario Giraldez, Academic Director, Alianza Cultural, Montevideo, Uruguay

REVIEWERS

BRAZIL

Renata Cardoso, Colégio do Sol, Guara, DF

Fábio Delano Vidal Carneiro, Colégio Sete de Setembro, Fortaleza

Cristiano Carvalho, Centro Educacional Leonardo da Vinci, Vitória

Silvia Corrêa, Associação Alumni, São Paulo

Carol Espinosa, Associação Cultural Brasil Estados Unidos, Salvador

Marcia Ferreira, Centro Cultural Brasil Estados Unidos, Franca

Clara Haddad, ELT Consultant, São Paulo

Elaine Carvalho Chaves Hodgson, Colégio Militar de Brasília, Brasília

Thays Farias Galvão Ladosky, Associação Brasil América, Recife

Itana Lins, Colégio Anchieta, Salvador

Samantha Mascarenhas, Associação Cultural Brasil Estados Unidos, Salvador

Ann Marie Moreira, Pan American School of Bahia, Bahia

Rodrigo Ramirez, CEETEPS- Fatec Zona Sul, São Paulo

Paulo Torres, Vitória Municipality, Vitória

Renata Zainotte, Go Up Idiomas, Rio de Janeiro

CHINA

Zhou Chao, MaxEn Education, Beijing

Zhu Haojun, Only International Education, Shanghai

Su Jing, Beijing Chengxun International English School, Beijing

Jianjun Shen, Phoenix City International School, Guangzhou

COSTA RICA

Luis Antonio Quesada-Umaña, Centro Cultural Costarricense Norteamericano, San José

INDONESIA

Luz S. Ismail, M.A., LIA Institute of Language and Vocational Training, Jakarta

Selestin Zainuddin, LIA Institute of Language and Vocational Training, Jakarta

Rosalia Dian Devitasari, SMP Kolese Kanisius, Jakarta

JAPAN

John Williams, Tezukayama Gakuen, Nara

MEXICO

Nefertiti González, Instituto Mexicano Madero, Puebla

Eugenia Islas, Instituto Tlalpan, Mexico City

Marta MM Seguí, Colegio Velmont A.C., Puebla

SOUTH KOREA

Min Yuol (Alvin) Cho, Global Leader English Education, Yong In

THAILAND

Panitnan Kalayanapong, Eduzone Co., Ltd., Bangkok

TURKEY

Damla Çaltuğ, İELEV, Istanbul

Basak Nalcakar Demiralp, Ankara Sinav College, Ankara

Humeyra Olcayli, İstanbul Bilim College, Istanbul

VIETNAM

Chantal Kruger, ILA Vietnam, Hô Chí Minh

Ai Nguyen Huynh, Vietnam USA Society, Hô Chí Minh

impact

3B

Unit 5

RYAN CARNEY Palaeontologist/Evolutionary Biologist

Ryan Carney's hero is Leonardo da Vinci. Most people know that da Vinci was a painter and an architect. Did you know that he also designed flying machines? Ryan is a little like his hero. He's also an artist, and studies the evolution of flight. Ryan examines flying dinosaurs and compares them with modern-day birds using x-ray machines.

Unit 6

BETHANY EHLMANN Planetary Geologist

Bethany Ehlmann studies planets and explores our solar system and beyond. She works on the NASA Mars Rover Curiosity mission. Bethany helps Curiosity navigate to collect rocks and minerals on Mars. She hopes we can study these samples to find signs of life on Mars and on other worlds. Do you believe there's life beyond Earth?

Unit 7

AMI VITALE National Geographic Photographer

Ami Vitale is more than just a photographer – she's a visual storyteller. Ami has visited more than 90 countries to take photographs. She's lived in mud huts, interacted with giant pandas and travelled through war zones. Ami thinks photos have the power to tell stories and create change. Do you enjoy taking photos? What story would you like to tell?

Unit 8

PAUL D. MILLER, AKA DJ SPOOKY Artist/Writer/Musician

Artist, writer and musician Paul D. Miller performs under the name DJ Spooky. He uses technology to create unique blends of sound for his songs. He's developed a DJ app to let others do the same. Paul looks at music as information, not just sound. He hopes his musical compositions can raise awareness about environmental and social issues.

Unit 5

TO START

1. We all know that birds fly. What other living things fly? Make a list of as many as you can.

2. Why do you think humans have always wanted to fly?

3. Would you like to be able to fly? Why or why not?

Jetmen flying over the city of Dubai, United Arab Emirates

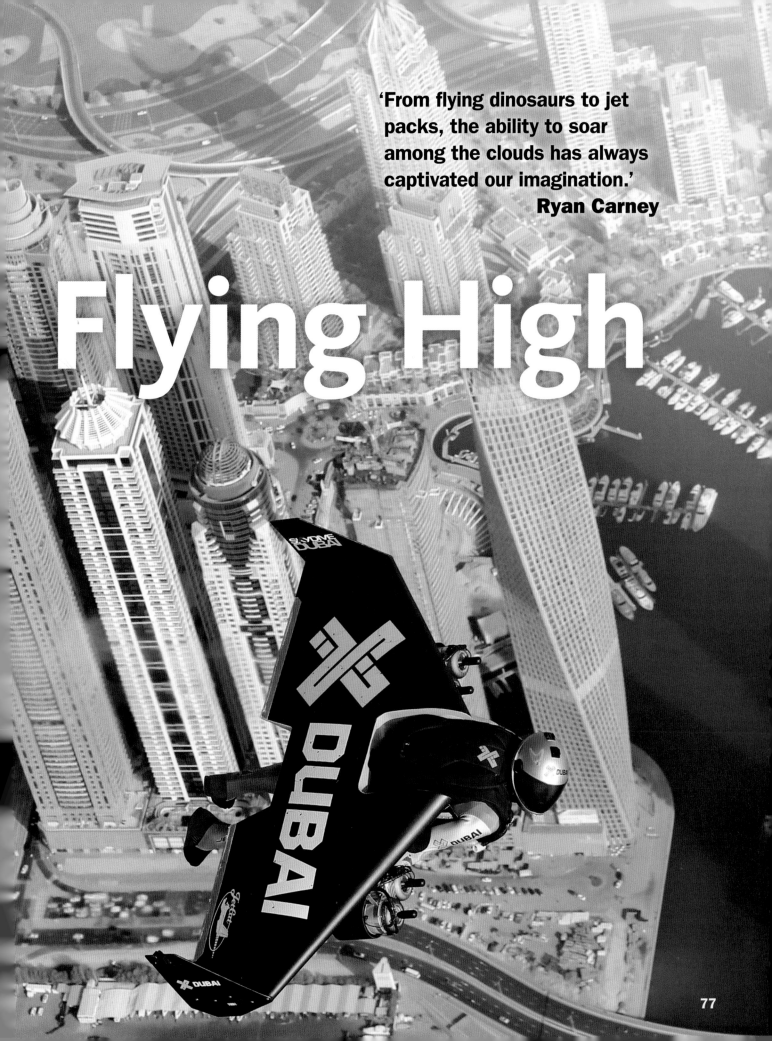

'From flying dinosaurs to jet packs, the ability to soar among the clouds has always captivated our imagination.'
Ryan Carney

Flying High

1 Which animal do you think was the first to fly? Why? Discuss. Then listen and read. ∩ 058

350 million years ago

Today it's hard to imagine an empty sky, but many millions of years ago, there was no **flight** of any kind. All life was **limited** to water or land. This included very **early** insects, which were the first animals to develop wings around 350 million years ago. How did wings **evolve**? The most accepted theory is that wings developed from structures that originally supported insects' ancestors as they moved in the water. Over time, these structures became larger and stronger. They turned into wings that first allowed insects to jump and then **glide**. Eventually, insects were able to **flap** their wings and fly.

229 million years ago

By 229 million years ago, flight had also developed in pterosaurs, large flying reptiles. These animals were not dinosaurs, but were closely related to them. They were good fliers because they had strong flight muscles, skin-covered wings and strong but **hollow** bones. They could glide, flap their wings and even **soar**, using the wind to help them stay in the air. The largest flying animal ever was a pterosaur named *Quetzalcoatlus*, which had a head as big as a human and a body as tall as a giraffe. *Quetzalcoatlus* had a **weight** of 200 kg. (440 lb.) and a **wingspan** of 11 m. (36 ft.)!

150 million years ago

Today's birds are actually living dinosaurs! The earliest known dinosaur that is generally considered to be the first bird is *Archaeopteryx*. It had feathered wings like modern birds, but also shared **features** with reptiles, such as teeth, clawed fingers and a bony tail. It could fly, but not very well. Later, birds became more skilled fliers due to better flight **adaptations**.

55 million years ago

The fourth and last appearance of flight happened 55 million years ago, when the ancestors of bats developed the **capability** of powered flight. It's likely that these mammals lived in trees and first became gliders. Over time, their bodies formed wings, making bats the only mammals that have evolved to fly.

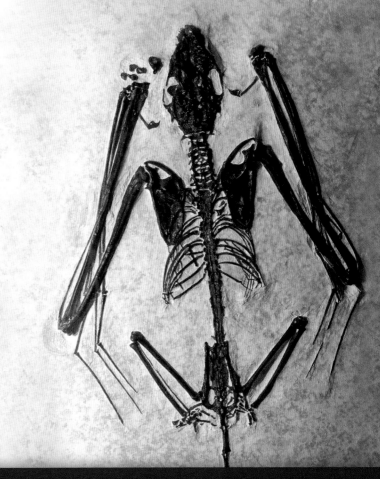

2 LEARN NEW WORDS **Listen and repeat.** 🎧 059

3 **Work in pairs.** The capability of flight has evolved in four groups: insects, pterosaurs, birds and bats. Why do you think each of these animals evolved to fly? How did it benefit them? Do you imagine any other animals evolving this way in the future? Explain.

Read and write the words from the list. Make any necessary changes.

adaptation	capability	evolve	flight
glide	hollow	limited	weight

As an evolutionary biologist and palaeontologist, Ryan Carney studies the history of dinosaurs and their modern-day descendants: birds. From a single feather, he was inspired to research the _____ that species made over time in order to fly. He is interested in *Archaeopteryx* because it was the earliest known dinosaur. *Archaeopteryx* was also the earliest species to _____ the _____ of powered flight. Ryan investigates the theory that _____ in birds originated from 'the ground up' (from ancestors that first ran on the ground), and not from 'the trees down' (from ancestors who lived in trees and then learnt to _____, before eventually flying).

Archaeopteryx feather fossil

Ryan Carney

5 **LEARN NEW WORDS Listen to these words and match them to their definitions.** Then listen and repeat. 🎧 060 061

allow	powered	skilled	support

_____ 1. to provide the capability to do something

_____ 2. having the capability to do something well

_____ 3. to carry the weight of something

_____ 4. having energy to produce movement

6 **YOU DECIDE Choose an activity. Work in pairs.**

1. List three insects that fly and three that don't. Compare the insects on the two lists. What are the advantages of flying for insects?

2. With around 10,000 species in existence, birds have developed a wide variety of adaptations for flight. Compare and contrast two very different-looking birds. How is their flight similar? How is it different?

3. Why do you think bats developed flight to use mainly at night? How are bats' flight adaptations different from those of other fliers?

Arguing	Conceding
I'm sure you agree that _____ .	I guess you have a point.
Well, I think that _____ .	
Most people support _____ .	Well, maybe you're right.
Yes, but what about _____ ?	

1 **Listen.** How do the speakers argue their points and concede? Write the phrases you hear. 🔊063

A colugo

2 **Read and complete the dialogue.**

Ann: You know, we still don't know much about the ancestors of bats. There just isn't much evidence.

Alan: Maybe, but _____ the idea that bats are closely related to a group of mammals that also includes the colugo.

Ann: Yes, _____ the fact that the colugo glides? It doesn't flap its wings and fly.

Alan: Well, I _____ bats and colugos probably had an ancestor in common at some point. Think about it. I'm

_____ that they share characteristics. Their wings look very similar. And both species eat insects. So it's logical that their ancestor would be a nocturnal glider who lived in trees.

Ann: I _____ there.

3 **Work in groups.** Cut out the cards. Take turns reading them aloud. Group members argue and concede each point.

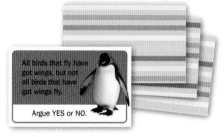

All birds that fly have got wings, but not all birds that have got wings fly.

Argue YES or NO.

Go to page 163.

4 **Work in pairs.** What affects your own life? What do you want to change? Take turns arguing and conceding.

Most students support the idea of less homework. I do, too.

Yes, but what about preparing for tests? Homework can be useful for that.

Well, maybe you're right.

GRAMMAR 🎧064

Past perfect: Talking about the first of two actions in the past

Pterosaurs disappeared.
Modern birds evolved.

Pterosaurs **had** already **disappeared** by the time modern birds evolved.

The capability of flight developed four times in animals.
Humans tried to fly.

By the time humans tried to fly, the capability of flight **had developed** in four groups of animals.

1 **Listen.** Which of the two actions in the past happened first? Tick the box. 🎧065

1. ☐ kite flight   ☐ animal flight
2. ☐ running, arm flapping   ☐ kite flight
3. ☐ measuring, signalling   ☐ human transport
4. ☐ fun and entertainment   ☐ military use
5. ☐ kites made of paper   ☐ kites made of silk

2 **Read and complete the sentences.** Use past perfect forms of the verbs in the box.

design	draw	forget	jump	run	try

    Jumping from towers, walls and cliffs was among many ways humans tried to fly. Many men _____ to fly like the birds before success was achieved in 875 CE. In that year, a man named Abdul Qasim Abbas Ibn Firnas jumped from a high wall built over a valley in Cordoba, Spain. Before his experiment, he _____ wings covered in feathers. He planned to wear them on his arms and legs. Also, he _____ on paper a series of wing movements to use in flight. According to the people who saw his experiment, he began to fall after he _____ . Afterwards, he climbed even higher than his starting point. He glided for several hundred feet, turned and came back to the wall. He hurt his back in the experiment, possibly because he _____ to include a tail in his design.

1000 BCE
The Chinese invent kites.

875 CE
Abbas Ibn Firnas wants to **prove** that man can fly. He tries flying by jumping with feathered wings.

1295
Marco Polo describes man-carrying kites.

3 **LEARN NEW WORDS Listen.** Learn about Leonardo da Vinci and the history of human flight. Then listen and repeat. 🎧 066 067

4 **Read the sentences.** Tick T for *true* or F for *false*.

1. Gravity is one of the forces that acts on flying and falling objects. (T) (F)
2. Leonardo da Vinci designed his parachute in 1595. (T) (F)
3. A stable flying object does not move from side to side. (T) (F)
4. Da Vinci created a helicopter that ascended into the sky at an angle. (T) (F)
5. A parachute can be used to help people descend safely from the sky. (T) (F)
6. Experts proved that da Vinci's glider was almost the same as Cayley's. (T) (F)

5 **Work in groups.** Use the timeline and new words to make four true sentences about flight. Use the past perfect.

1. _____
   _____

2. _____
   _____

3. _____
   _____

4. _____
   _____

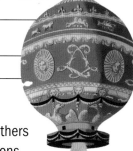

1485
Leonardo da Vinci studies **forces** that affect objects in the air in order to design flying machines.

1595
Fausto Veranzio designs a **parachute**.

1670
Francesco Lana de Terzi designs an airship.

1783
The Montgolfier brothers launch hot-air balloons. These balloons **ascend** when the air inside is hot and **descend** when it cools.

1800
George Cayley designs the first **stable** glider to carry a human.

1 BEFORE YOU READ **Discuss in pairs.** What do you know about the Wright brothers and flight? Make a list. What are three facts you expect to find in the reading?

2 **LEARN NEW WORDS Find the words in the reading.** What do you think they mean? Then find the words *land*, *fuel* and *pilot* in a dictionary. Look at the different ways these words can be used. Then listen and repeat all of the new words. 🎧 068

| engine | fuel | to land | pilot | to take off |

3 WHILE YOU READ **Notice the order in which events happened.** 🎧 069

Reaching FOR THE Sky

The Dream of Human Flight

One day while travelling, Milton Wright saw a small toy helicopter that was powered by rubber bands. He bought this toy for his two young sons, Orville and Wilbur. Mr Wright surely had no idea this simple act would lead to the creation of the world's first powered aeroplane. The toy gave the brothers a strong interest in flight. They soon began trying to build similar models themselves.

When they were older, the Wright brothers decided they wanted to make a 'small contribution' to the field of flight. At that time, most attention on flight focused on hot-air balloons and gliders. However, the brothers were more interested in a heavier flying machine, powered by an engine and controlled by a pilot. They first read all the books they could on the early mechanics of flight. Then they used kites to better understand the forces that controlled objects in the air.

Over the next three years, the Wright brothers worked on designs and shapes for different types of gliders. During this time, they worked with engineers Otto Lilienthal and Octave Chanute, both authors of books on flight. These men were important influences on the brothers' work.

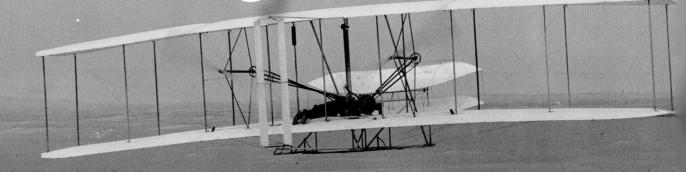

In December 1903, Orville Wright takes off with his brother Wilbur running beside him.

The brothers had built a wind tunnel to test different shapes of wings and tails for their gliders. Then they began to think about how to get a flying machine weighing 272 kg. (600 lb.) into the air and keep it there. They designed a 12-horsepower engine that generated enough force to allow the Flyer to take off from the ground in December 1903. It ascended about 3 m. (10 ft.) into the air and continued to fly 36 m. (120 ft.) in about 12 seconds. The first heavier-than-air flight became a reality!

The second, third and fourth flights followed on the same day. But the Wright brothers observed that the Flyer was not stable enough and was hard to control. They spent two more years perfecting their aeroplane. Finally, on the 5th of October 1905, Flyer III flew about 39 km. (24 mi.) in 39 minutes. The plane landed only because it ran out of fuel. The dream of human flight had finally come true.

1891
Otto Lilienthal builds a glider.

1894
Octave Chanute's book on flying machines is published.

1891
Samuel Langley creates his aerodrome model.

1901
Alberto Santos-Dumont circles the Eiffel Tower.

1905
The Wright brothers fly for 39 minutes in Flyer III.

4 AFTER YOU READ **Work in pairs to answer the questions.**

1. What is the main idea of the reading?

2. How did the Wright brothers prepare for their project?

3. Whose ideas on flight influenced the Wright brothers?

4. The Wright brothers worked on their flight project for years. What personality characteristics do you think they had that helped them reach their goals?

5 **Put the events in order.**

_____ The Wright brothers built a wind tunnel to test the wings and tails of their gliders.

_____ They read everything they could about flight.

_____ They flew Flyer III about 39 km. (24 mi.) before it ran out of fuel.

_____ They designed a 12-horsepower engine to power the Flyer.

___1___ They used kites to learn more about how things fly.

_____ They worked for two years to make the Flyer more stable.

6 **Discuss in groups.**

1. How do you think the Wright brothers' work helped shape the 20th century? What aspects of life changed?

2. Is just one person ever truly responsible for a great idea or invention? Do all ideas and inventions build on the work of previous generations? What do you think? Why?

VIDEO▶

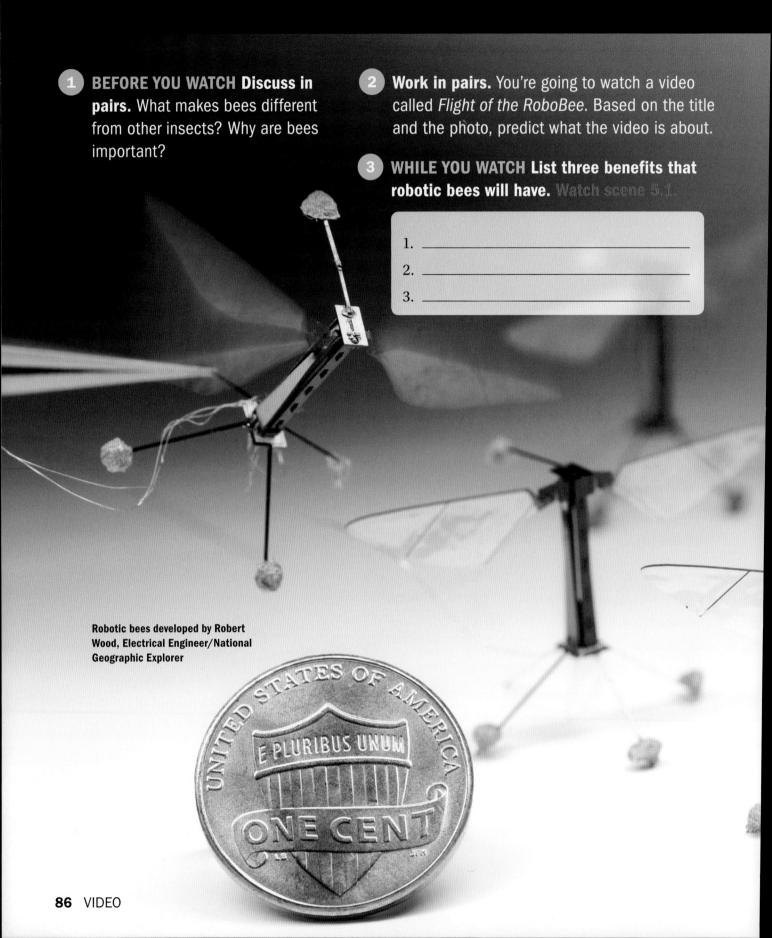

1 **BEFORE YOU WATCH Discuss in pairs.** What makes bees different from other insects? Why are bees important?

2 **Work in pairs.** You're going to watch a video called *Flight of the RoboBee*. Based on the title and the photo, predict what the video is about.

3 **WHILE YOU WATCH List three benefits that robotic bees will have.** Watch scene 5.1.

1. _____

2. _____

3. _____

Robotic bees developed by Robert Wood, Electrical Engineer/National Geographic Explorer

4 **AFTER YOU WATCH** **Work in pairs to decide if each sentence is *true* or *false*.** Tick the correct answer.

1. Robert Wood says that most new robots are large, powerful and dangerous. (T) (F)

2. Robert's robots are inspired by nature. (T) (F)

3. Robert looks at real insects to work out how to construct his robotic bees. (T) (F)

4. Robotic bees haven't got the supports necessary to fly independently. (T) (F)

5. Robert doesn't plan to send robotic bees into dangerous areas because they could break. (T) (F)

6. Getting the robots to fly was a long, difficult process for Robert and his team. (T) (F)

5 **Discuss in groups.** In the video, Robert says, 'If you don't fail, you don't learn enough.' Explain what you think he means by this.

6 **Work in groups.** You learnt about man's early attempts at flying. Compare and contrast the process of getting the robotic bee to fly with the processes of the flight pioneers you learnt about.

7 **YOU DECIDE** **Choose an activity.**

1. **Work independently.** Research other robotic insects that are being developed. Choose one and create a short presentation on it. Explain what it's used for. Compare it with the robotic bee.

2. **Work in pairs.** Robert says that robotics is 'the next big thing to impact our lives'. Find an example of a robot that is making an impact on people's lives. Write an article about this robot and the impact it's having.

3. **Work in groups.** Create a poster to advertise robotic bees. Use illustrations and text to describe them, and explain why they are useful.

GRAMMAR 🎧070

Past perfect continous: Talking about the first of two actions in the past

The Wright brothers **had been working** on powered flight for several years before Wilbur Wright flew for 2 hours and 19 minutes in 1908.

Before Louis Bleriot first crossed the English Channel in an aeroplane in 1909, pilots **had been using** hot-air balloons.

1 **Read.** Complete the sentences with past perfect continuous forms of the verbs in brackets.

1. Otto Lilienthal _____ (use) gliders for around five years before he crashed in one in 1896.

2. Before Samuel Langley's large Aerodrome A crashed while taking off, he _____ (build) smaller machines that flew successfully.

3. Before Alberto Santos-Dumont made the first successful powered flight in Europe, he _____ (win) awards for his flights in balloons.

4. Engineer Frank Whittle _____ (work) on his theories for nine years before he tested his first jet engine in 1937.

5. Before Charles Yeager became the first pilot to travel faster than the speed of sound in 1947, he _____ (fly) for about five years.

Charles Yeager

2 **Work in pairs.** Take turns throwing the cube. Ask and answer questions. Use the past perfect continuous.

Before you became part of the (group/team), how long _____ you _____ ?

Before modern aeroplanes appeared, how long _____ inventors _____ ?

Before you started this class, how long _____ you _____ ?

Before you became part of the team, how long had you been playing basketball?

I had been playing basketball for six years.

Go to page 165.

WRITING

When we classify, we organise our ideas into categories. First, we introduce the topic. Then we divide it into categories. Each category gets its own paragraph in the essay. In each paragraph, we describe shared characteristics that make up that category. A classification essay ends with a conclusion. In the conclusion, we bring the categories back together to talk about the main topic.

1 **Read the model.** Work in pairs to identify the categories and details.

Long before we had aeroplanes, people had been experimenting with different flying machines. We still use some of those flying machines today. Some depend on air for movement, while others use engines.

Hot-air balloons and gliders use air currents for movement. Hot-air balloon pilots steer their aircraft by ascending or descending into air currents that move the balloon. The pilot controls the balloon's movement by heating the air inside the balloon, or by allowing it to cool naturally.

A glider also uses air currents to soar and glide. Small planes pull gliders along a runway to help them take off. But once in the air, gliders use the currents, not an engine, to move. Their long wingspan and strong body give riders a safe, smooth flight. Hot-air balloons and gliders are most often used for fun and adventure.

Helicopters first appeared during World War II. A helicopter hasn't got wings, but, like an aeroplane, it's got an engine that makes its blades spin at high speeds. This allows the helicopter to ascend into the sky. Unlike an aeroplane, which has to keep moving, helicopters can stay in one place in the sky for a long time. Today, helicopters are mostly used by medical teams and the military. But you can also take a helicopter ride for fun. Many tourist destinations offer helicopter rides for sightseeing.

So before your next plane ride, remember that planes aren't the only way to fly.

2 **Work in pairs.** What does the writer classify? How many categories are there? What details are mentioned in each part?

3 **Write.** Write a classification essay to describe two types of animal flight.

NATIONAL GEOGRAPHIC

Explore Your Interests

'As an evolutionary biologist, I get to combine both childhood interests into my research: dinosaurs and animation!'

Ryan Carney

National Geographic Explorer, Palaeontologist/Evolutionary Biologist

1. **Watch scene 5.2.**

2. What are your interests? How have they changed over the years? Is there anything that you were interested in as a child that you are still learning about? What is it?

3. The people you read about in this unit, from Leonardo da Vinci to Ryan Carney, made their interests their life's work. How could you turn your own interests into a career? What would you need to do?

Make an Impact

YOU DECIDE Choose a project.

1 **Design a flying machine.**

- Plan and design a flying machine.
- Use your plans to create a model of the machine.
- Present your machine to the class. Explain how it works.

2 **Make an evolution poster.**

- Choose an animal that has evolved the capability of flight.
- Research how this animal has evolved over time. Draw and label at least four steps in its evolution.
- Arrange your drawings in order on a poster. Display the poster in class.

3 **Advertise a flying machine.**

- Choose a flying machine that you learnt about.
- Think about the benefits and risks of using that machine.
- Make an advertisement for the machine. Try to persuade your audience to fly in it.

A pilot guiding a home-made machine during a flying competition in Moscow, Russia

New Frontiers

'We are pushing the frontiers in our own solar system, sending missions to other worlds, looking outward to distant pinpoints of light.'
Bethany Ehlmann

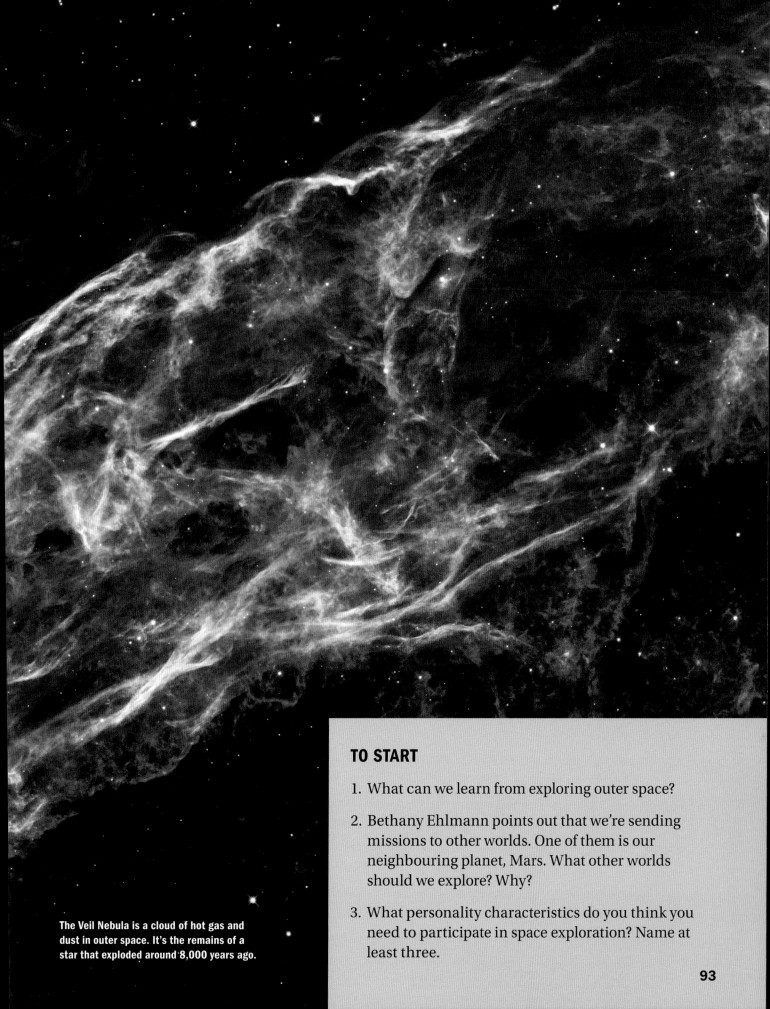

The Veil Nebula is a cloud of hot gas and dust in outer space. It's the remains of a star that exploded around 8,000 years ago.

TO START

1. What can we learn from exploring outer space?

2. Bethany Ehlmann points out that we're sending missions to other worlds. One of them is our neighbouring planet, Mars. What other worlds should we explore? Why?

3. What personality characteristics do you think you need to participate in space exploration? Name at least three.

1 **Recent space exploration has focused on Mars. Why do you think this is?**
Discuss. Then listen and read. 🎧 071

We think of Earth as the *Blue Planet* and Mars as the *Red Planet* when looking at **satellite** images of them. Although they look very different, our home planet and Mars are actually similar in many **aspects**. Like Earth, Mars has its own **atmosphere** and clouds. Both planets have large, ice-covered areas called *polar caps*. Mars's **landscape** includes features also found on Earth, such as mountains, **plains**, channels, craters and even volcanoes.

Both planets have days that are about 24 hours long, and both spin on an invisible line called an *axis*. Each planet tilts to the side on its axis, at an angle of about 24 **degrees** in relation to the sun. This tilt is what causes the seasons to change on both planets.

The Curiosity rover on the surface of Mars

Astronomers have always **wondered** if life exists beyond Earth. If it does, our neighbour Mars is the most likely place to find it. Mars is a planet of wild extremes. It has the largest **dust** storms, the deepest and longest **valley**, the highest mountain and the largest volcano known in our solar system! But to most planetary scientists, the biggest question is whether life is, or was, possible on the planet.

Advances in technology have allowed scientists to equip robots with a variety of tools and then send them to explore Mars. These scientific **instruments** have been able to **detect** real **proof** that life is possible there. For example, one of the **fundamental** requirements for life, the existence of some form of water, has been discovered in several areas of Mars. A **vast** amount of ice is under the surface and also frozen in the polar caps year-round. In 2015, scientists confirmed that liquid water exists on Mars's surface. But will this finding **lead to** the discovery of life on the Red Planet? We're still waiting to find out.

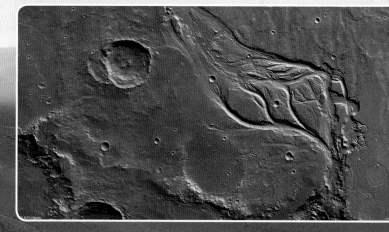

Channels on Mars's surface suggest the presence of water.

2 **LEARN NEW WORDS Listen and repeat.**
🎧 072

3 **Work in pairs.** Why is it important that scientists find proof of water on Mars? Do you think that they will find life on the Red Planet? Why or why not?

4 Read and circle the correct word.

As a planetary geologist, Bethany Ehlmann studies our solar system. She *wonders* / *leads to* how the rocks on Mars were formed and how they interacted with water. She also is looking for *degrees* / *proof* that life could have been or could be present on the Red Planet. She works closely with Curiosity, a six-wheeled robot called a *rover*. Rovers can move around and explore. Curiosity travels through the plains and *valleys* / *aspects* on the surface of Mars. It uses scientific *dust* / *instruments* to analyse the Martian *proof* / *landscape*. Bethany hopes that Curiosity's work, combined with new technological advances, will one day provide the answer to the *fundamental* / *satellite* question: Is there life beyond Earth?

5 LEARN NEW WORDS Listen to these words and match them to the definitions. Then listen and repeat. 🎧 073 074

advance	astronomer	equip with	requirement

_____ 1. to provide

_____ 2. progress in science or technology

_____ 3. something that's necessary

_____ 4. a person who studies the stars and planets

Bethany Ehlmann with a Mars rover

6 YOU DECIDE Choose an activity.

1. **Work independently.** Go online to learn more about the Curiosity rover's mission. Write a paragraph about what you learnt.

2. **Work in pairs.** Make a Venn diagram. Compare and contrast Earth and Mars.

3. **Work in groups.** Hundreds of years ago, adventurers spent years exploring countries and continents, leaving everything they knew behind them. If you knew you would spend years away, and maybe never return, would you explore Mars? Why or why not? Discuss with your group. Then share with the class.

Speculating

Do you think that <u>they'll ever find life on Mars</u>?	Most likely, <u>scientists will research the topic for a long time</u>.
	I'll bet <u>they're close to finding life</u>!
	It's likely that <u>they'll first find microbes</u>.
What if <u>scientists really do find evidence of life</u>?	I'm fairly sure that <u>will change everything</u>!

1 **Listen.** How do the speakers speculate? Write the phrases you hear. ⋒076

2 **Read and complete the dialogue.**

Mia: I just read a really interesting article about the Curiosity rover on Mars. By examining the soil, it helped scientists learn more about ancient Mars.

Lee: Well, _____ they had to dig really deep to find soil and rocks from ancient times.

Mia: That's not true. The article said that 50 per cent of the rock on Mars's surface is from ancient times.

Lee: So _____ that scientists can really learn much from studying some old rocks?

Mia: Well, yes. _____ these rocks hold information about the possibility of life on Mars. The samples that Curiosity collected show that the chemicals needed to support life were present on the planet.

Lee: _____ Curiosity discovers living creatures on Mars?

Mia: _____ , we won't see photos of little green Martians, if that's what you mean. _____ if Curiosity can find proof of life, it will be microscopic organisms found in the icy regions.

3 **Work in pairs.** Take a card and look at the photo from Mars. Speculate about what you see. Your partner will read the correct information. Then swap roles.

What if this is food growing on Mars? I'll bet they'll try sending some back to Earth.

Actually they're mineral balls found on Mars's surface. I'm fairly sure that we won't want to eat them!

4 **Work in groups.** Speculate about the near future. How well are you going to do on your next test? How well is your favourite sports team going to do this year? How soon are you going to make a new good friend?

Round balls of minerals found on Mars

Go to page 167.

Present and past conditionals: Talking about unlikely (but possible) or impossible situations

Unlikely but possible

If I **were** a scientist, I **would focus** my research on Saturn.

He **would be** a space tourist if he **had** the money.

Impossible

If I **had known** there was a talk about Mars, I **would have gone**.

They **could have fixed** the rover if they **had equipped** it with better tools.

Habitable by Humans?

The planet Saturn is made up of gas, so it doesn't have a **habitable** environment. If scientists wanted to find life around Saturn, they would have better luck studying two of its moons: Enceladus and Titan.

---

1 **Listen.** What's the reality in each case? Tick the box. 🔊078

1.	☐ I'm not president.	☐	I'm president.
2.	☐ The project succeeded.	☐	The project failed.
3.	☐ I investigated Titan.	☐	I didn't investigate Titan.
4.	☐ There is one space station.	☐	There are two space stations.
5.	☐ We repeated the experiment.	☐	We didn't repeat the experiment.
6.	☐ I don't explore space.	☐	I explore space.

2 **Read.** Complete the sentences with the correct form of the verbs in brackets.

Saturn has always been a fascinating planet. At about 1.2 billion km. (746 million mi.) from Earth, it was the most distant of the worlds recognised by ancient sky watchers. If they _____ (study) it the way we are able to today, they _____ (be) amazed. They _____ (find) that its rings consisted of billions of icy particles. They _____ (discover) that these rings are extremely thin – only 10 m. (33 ft.) thick. And they _____ (learn) that some of the planet's small moons play an important part in controlling the orbits and spacing of the rings. If you _____ (study) Saturn's moons today, you _____ (observe) that some of its 62 moons orbit in opposite directions. You _____ (see) that some moons even exchange orbits. Most importantly, you _____ (learn) that two of the moons have the potential for life!

ENCELADUS
- 500 km. (311 mi.) in diameter
- one day = 1.37 Earth days
- temperature: −201°C (−330°F)
- atmosphere: very thin
- no weather
- **geysers** that send water vapour and pieces of ice into the sky

TITAN
- 2,575 km. (1,600 mi.) in **diameter**
- one day = 16 Earth days
- temperature: −179°C (−290°F)
- atmosphere: thick and **hazy**
- **seasonal** storm cycles
- surface lakes, seas of liquid methane

4 **Work independently.** Imagine you spent a year living on Titan and are now back home on Earth, telling a friend about it. Complete the sentences with present or past conditionals.

1. If you _____ (have) the right equipment, you
   _____ (visit) Titan and be able to experience life on a moon.

2. If you _____ (come) to Titan while I was there, would you
   _____ (swim) with me in a surface lake?

3. If I _____ (know) you would be living on Titan, I
   _____ (remind) you about the seasonal storm cycles.

4. If I _____ (be) on Titan today, I _____
   (try) to take photographs of the storms.

5. If Enceladus _____ (be) habitable by humans, I
   _____ (go) there next year.

6. If I _____ (go) to Enceladus, I _____
   (study) the geysers.

5 **Work in groups.** If you had to visit one of these two moons, which one would you choose? Why? Give two or three reasons.

> If I could travel to one of Saturn's moons, I'd go to Enceladus to see the geysers.

More Than a Dream

1 BEFORE YOU READ Discuss in pairs.
When we think of space, we think of astronauts. But there are many other types of jobs in any space mission. Other than astronauts, what other kinds of space-related jobs can you think of?

2 LEARN NEW WORDS Find these words in the reading. What do you think they mean? Think about the parts of each word. Use a dictionary to check. Then listen and repeat. ∩ 081

aspiring	background	chance
leadership	perseverance	

3 WHILE YOU READ Think about the different categories that the information can be organised into. ∩ 082

4 AFTER YOU READ Work in pairs to answer the questions.

1. What is the main purpose of the reading?

2. Who is Alyssa Carson? Why is she mentioned in the reading?

3. What do you think happens at a space camp session?

4. Besides camp, what can aspiring astronauts do to prepare for space?

Astronauts-in-training testing a surface transport vehicle in the desert

Could space be your own new frontier?

Are you one of Earth's next generation of explorer-astronauts? What do aspiring astronauts do to prepare for the possibility of a career in space?

A good person to ask would be Alyssa Carson. Her dream is to be the first person on Mars. As a child, Alyssa read as much as possible about Mars, studied its maps, and did everything she could to learn about the Red Planet. This included going to a space-themed camp for the first time at age seven. Since then, Alyssa has attended more than 20 such camps. In fact, at age 13 she was the first person ever to complete all the NASA Space Camps in the world. At these camps, future astronauts get the chance to ride in space-flight simulators and experience what zero gravity feels like.

While Space Camp may not be possible for everyone, there are many other ways to prepare for a future in space. If you're interested, consider the following:

- Astronauts must be in excellent physical condition. Now's the time to begin a healthy lifestyle of a balanced diet, regular exercise and plenty of sleep.

- Astronauts need to meet a wide range of physical challenges. Skills acquired through activities such as scuba diving, skydiving, skiing, mountain climbing and piloting aircraft are extremely valuable. Now's a great time to start learning these types of skills little by little.

- Astronauts need to meet a wide range of emotional challenges. Work on developing positive traits, such as patience, co-operation and perseverance. Take every opportunity to practise team-building, leadership and problem-solving skills.

- Astronauts need to have a strong background in maths and science. Work with your school's advisers and mentors to determine the best subjects to study. Keep up with real-time developments and discoveries in space.

- Don't forget languages! In addition to English, you'll need to know other languages such as Russian and Chinese to communicate successfully.

Alyssa Carson

5 **Work in pairs.** Classify the types of challenges astronauts face. Give examples of each type.

6 **Discuss in groups.**

1. Of the challenges astronauts face, which do you think are the hardest? Why?

2. Alyssa Carson is preparing for her dream career as an astronaut. What's your dream career? What can you do now to prepare for it?

3. One day, humans may live in space colonies. What would an ordinary family's typical day be like in a space colony? Would you like to live in a space colony? Why or why not?

VIDEO ▶

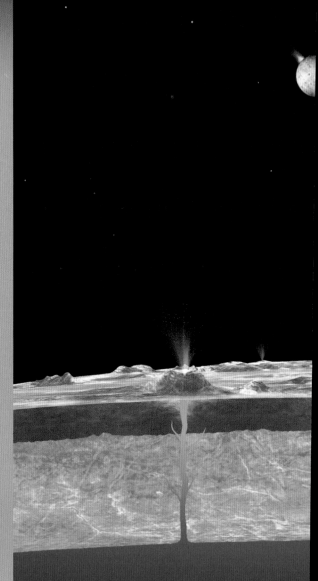

This illustration shows what scientists believe is a global liquid ocean under Europa's surface. Jupiter (right) and another of its 67 moons, Io, are in the background.

1 BEFORE YOU WATCH **Discuss in pairs.** You've learnt about the possibility of life beyond Earth. What are three characteristics of places where life is considered to be possible?

2 **Read and circle.** The video you're going to watch is called *Europa: Ocean World.* Based on what you've learnt in this unit, predict what the video will be about. Circle the correct letter.

a. another world with an ocean

b. an ocean near Europe

c. a new world discovered by Europeans

3 WHILE YOU WATCH **Think about the requirements for life.** Circle the ones you hear mentioned in the video. Watch scene 6.1.

energy	gases
liquid water	plants
substances found in rocks	warm temperatures

4 AFTER YOU WATCH **Work in pairs.** Circle the correct answer.

1. Kevin Hand says that life on Earth may have begun in our *oceans / caves*.

2. Where you find liquid *lava / water*, you generally find life.

3. Europa's ocean has existed for *ten thousand / billions of* years.

4. *Earth / Europa* has more water and deeper oceans.

5. Scientists used to think that for a world to be habitable, it had to be *the right distance from / in orbit around* the sun.

6. Now scientists realise that life is possible wherever there are the key elements for life: water, energy and the building blocks found in *plants / rocks*.

5 **Work in pairs.** You've learnt about three moons so far in this unit. Compare and contrast Europa with Titan and Enceladus. How are they the same? How are they different? Create a diagram to show your ideas.

6 **Work in groups.** To answer the question of whether there is life in Europa's oceans, scientists must collect information from those oceans. Name two challenges scientists face in gathering that information.

7 **YOU DECIDE** **Choose an activity.**

1. **Work independently.** Learn more about Europa. Use the information you collect to design and label a model of Europa. Present it to the class.

2. **Work in pairs.** Imagine that life has just been discovered on Europa. Write and illustrate a newspaper article explaining how that happened and what was found.

3. **Work in groups.** Imagine you work for a research group that studies Europa and you're trying to get people to support your work. Prepare and give a presentation explaining why it's important to study Europa. Persuade your audience to support your work.

Adverbs: Comparing how things are done

The new satellite transmits data **efficiently**.

The last satellite didn't transmit data **as efficiently as** the new satellite.

The new satellite transmits data **more efficiently than** the last satellite.

The new satellite transmits data **the most efficiently** of all the satellites.

The new rover travels **fast**.

The last rover didn't travel **as fast as** the new rover.

The new rover travels **faster than** the last rover.

The new rover travels **the fastest** of all the rovers.

1 **Complete the sentences.** Use the correct form of the adverbs in brackets.

Astronomers had dreamt of a telescope that would photograph the universe _____ (clearly) than telescopes on the ground could. That dream came true in 1990 when the Hubble Space Telescope was launched into orbit _____ (approximately) 612 km. (380 mi.) above the Earth.

Hubble has photographed some of _____ (spectacularly) beautiful images of space ever taken. But that's not all. It has _____ (greatly) expanded our knowledge of space. Before Hubble, astronomers could not estimate the age of the universe _____ (precisely) they can now. Because of what they've seen through Hubble, astronomers have estimated that the universe is around 14 billion years old.

What's after Hubble? The Webb Space Telescope, which will measure distant objects even _____ (accurately) than Hubble.

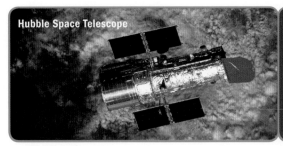

Hubble Space Telescope

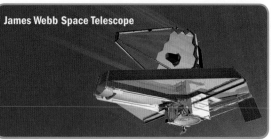

James Webb Space Telescope

2 **Work in groups.** Spin each wheel. Take turns comparing how group members do or have done different activities using the words from each spinner.

I have been speaking English as long as you.

Yes, but Camille has been speaking English the longest!

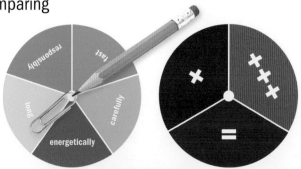

responsibly · fast · carefully · energetically · long

104 GRAMMAR

Go to page 165.

WRITING

One way to organise persuasive writing is to present both sides of an argument, point by point. First describe one argument and then present a counter-argument in the same paragraph. Do the same for additional arguments, presenting counter-arguments each time.

1 **Read the model.** Work in pairs to circle one side of the writer's argument and underline the counter-argument. Do this for each point.

It's extremely important to develop new technology wisely, so that everyone can benefit from it. Some people believe our technology plan should focus on building spacecraft. Others believe it should focus on building robots. Which is the better course of action?

For those who dream of exploring outer space, the development of high-tech spacecraft is essential. But just one spaceship costs billions of dollars more to build than even the most complex robot. Many specialised robots could be designed and built much more cheaply than spaceships, and they could be used for practical purposes right here on Earth.

Many of the people who focus on future space exploration describe solving key mysteries of space and perhaps even the origin of life in the universe. While this kind of knowledge is fascinating, there are no practical benefits from it for people on Earth right now. Robots will have new applications in the future, but even the robots we currently have benefit us in practical ways. For example, they can work in dangerous conditions, such as places with extreme temperatures. They can take apart bombs, build products or perform complex surgery – all useful things that benefit people right now.

To sum up, it's clearly better to give attention, time and money to the technological development of robots. They are less expensive to develop and more useful. Robots also benefit people in ways that are more practical than any benefit from a spacecraft.

2 **Work in pairs.** In your opinion, which of the two positions on technological development is more persuasive? Why?

3 **Write.** Write about the argument that it's better to explore the ocean than outer space. Present both sides of the argument and persuade your readers to agree with you.

A flying robot that may be used for security, rescue and even space exploration

Discover the Future

'Technology development is a huge part of our exploration and our ability to access the stories and the discoveries on other worlds.'

Bethany Ehlmann
National Geographic Explorer, Planetary Geologist

1. **Watch scene 6.2.**

2. Bethany uses technology to explore Mars without being there. Where else can you explore using only technology?

3. Do you believe that people will live on Mars in the future? Why or why not? What would be the advantages and disadvantages of creating a colony there?

Make an Impact

YOU DECIDE Choose a project.

1 **Design and write a postcard from outer space.**

- Research one of the places mentioned in this unit to learn more about it.
- Imagine you took a week-long journey to this place. Write a postcard message about your trip. Include information on travelling to and from your destination.
- Find a photo of the place. Create your postcard by sticking your photo on one side and your message on the other.

2 **Plan a space mission.**

- Choose a place in outer space that you would like to explore.
- Design a space mission to explore that place. Write about what you would need and what you would want to find out about.
- Give a speech to the class presenting your idea. Persuade your listeners to support your mission.

3 **Create an outer-space TV programme.**

- Write a script for a TV programme whose characters live in outer space.
- Work in groups to rehearse the script.
- Film your programme and share it with the class.

Express Yourself

1 **Read and listen to a scene from a film script about a team of space explorers.** 🎧 084

```
FADE IN:
EXTERIOR SPACESHIP IN ORBIT AROUND MARS

FADE TO:
INTERIOR SPACESHIP MAIN CONTROL ROOM - NIGHT

MARK and SONIA, with torches on, come through the
doors and stop in front of a bank of dimly lit
active computer screens.

                    MARK
          OK, we're here alone. Now show me
               what you're talking about.

                    SONIA
           Look at screen seventeen.
           Something strange is going on.

                    MARK
           I don't see anything unusual.

                    SONIA
           Look at the top right corner.

Mark catches his breath as he leans in to examine
the top right corner of the computer screen.

                    MARK
           (turning to look wildly at Sonia)
                That's impossible!

                    SONIA
           I know. But it's there.
```

MARK
I can't believe it! We need to wake up
the mission commander right now.

Sonia puts her hand firmly on Mark's shoulder.

SONIA
Don't panic. We need to think.

MARK
Are you joking?
What's there to think about?

Sonia takes a deep breath. Then she looks directly
into Mark's eyes.

SONIA
Mark, I don't trust him.

2 **Work in groups.** In this scene, two astronauts
see something very unusual on their screen. What
do you think they see? List three possibilities.
Then compare your ideas with those of another
group. Are your ideas similar? Which idea is the
most surprising?

3 **Connect ideas.** In Unit 5, you learnt about the
history of flight. In Unit 6, you learnt about space
exploration. How did the early pioneers of flight
set the stage for space exploration? Discuss the
evolution of flight that led to spacecraft.

4 **YOU DECIDE** **Choose an activity.**

1. Choose a topic:
   • flight
   • space exploration

2. Choose a way to express yourself:
   • the next scene of the film script
   • a presentation on flight (including spacecraft)
   • an original film or play

3. Present your work.

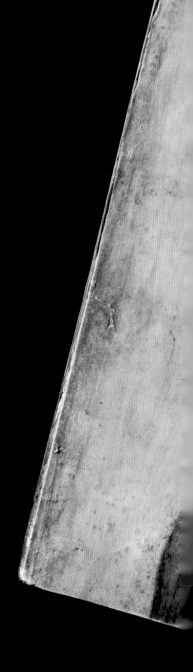

Visual Stories

'Photography and filmmaking are very powerful ways to give people other ideas and other things to think about.'

Ami Vitale

TO START

1. The title of this unit is *Visual Stories*. Look at the photograph. What story does it tell?

2. Photographer Ami Vitale uses photography to give people new ideas and new things to think about. Should this be the goal of all photographers? Why or why not?

3. In addition to photography and filmmaking, what other kinds of visual arts tell stories?

A museum worker moves *La Bella Principessa*, which many believe was painted by Leonardo da Vinci.

1 **Why are stories important? How are they told?** Discuss. Then listen and read. ∩ 085

Stories have been a **meaningful** form of communication throughout human history. Do you remember a time when a family member told you a story without reading it from a book? **Oral** stories are a part of every culture, and they allow us to pass traditions and values from one generation to the next. **Visual** stories have also been told in a variety of ways for thousands of years. Researchers have found rocks that were decorated by humans more than 100,000 years ago. Although the rocks had only simple linear patterns, the patterns had meaning. And it's meaning that creates a story.

People began painting on cave walls around 40,000 years ago. As time went on, painted **images** appeared on everything from pottery to **canvas**. Painting is a fairly permanent way to **represent** information. Because painted walls and objects have lasted for thousands of years, they give us a window into the past. Through this window we can see the stories of ancient Egyptians on the walls of their tombs. We can also see **scenes** from Renaissance Europe, showing the lives of people from kings to commoners. These paintings allow us to be **witnesses** to history.

In the early 19th century, French artist Louis-Jacques-Mande Daguerre introduced a device that provided another way to tell visual stories: the *daguerreotype*. This early camera was first used to take **portraits**. Photography with other subjects eventually became popular, but it took a while. At first people were afraid of a camera's ability to capture real life!

Today, photographers like Ami Vitale use photos to **portray** how people live. Ami presents her photos in ways that create certain responses from her **audience**, such as **anger** or **shock**. 'Photography creates change,' she says. Ami hopes that by telling her **subjects'** stories visually, she'll get people to realise that we're more alike than we are different. This will create a greater **understanding** among people around the world.

Visual stories are told on the walls of the tomb of Queen Hatshepsut, Egypt.

2 **LEARN NEW WORDS Listen and repeat.**
   🎧 086

3 **Work in pairs.** Have you got a favourite painting? A favourite photograph? Describe one, and the story it tells, to your partner.

4 **Read and write the words from the list.** Make any necessary changes.

anger	audience	meaningful	portrait	portray
scene	subject	understanding	visual	witness

Ami Vitale is known for the way she _____ international news and culture in her photos. Ami worries that some people may not have a good _____ of one another's cultures, so she creates _____ stories to make us think about how we see others. She believes that photographs can make us _____ to things that we wouldn't see otherwise. Photos can show people and places in a _____ new way. Ami wants her _____ to look closely at her powerful photos and feel more connected to their _____, even if they then feel emotions like _____ or sadness.

5 **LEARN NEW WORDS Listen to these words and match them to their definitions.** Then listen and repeat. 🎧 087 088

Ami Vitale

capture	certain	last	permanent

_____ 1. to record something in pictures or words

_____ 2. particular, specific

_____ 3. never ends or goes away

_____ 4. to exist over time

6 **YOU DECIDE Choose an activity.**

1. **Work independently.** Research cave paintings or images from Egyptian tombs. Choose a selection and write a paragraph to describe the story it tells.

2. **Work in pairs.** Bring a photo from home that you feel tells a clear story. Ask your partner to tell the story he/she sees in your photo. Then tell your partner the real story.

3. **Work in groups.** Who are some well-known painters in your country? Do their paintings tell stories? If so, what stories do they tell? Discuss.

SPEAKING STRATEGY 🎧089

Explaining a process

First, <u>you need to find a good camera</u>.

The next step is <u>choosing a good location</u>.

After that, <u>you need to pack the right equipment</u>.

Next, <u>check the weather</u>!

Meanwhile, <u>check to see that you have enough space on your computer</u>.

Make sure you <u>save your photos when you've finished</u>.

1 **Listen.** How does the speaker explain the process of sharing photos? Write the phrases you hear. 🎧090

2 **Read and complete the dialogue.**

Aki: Hi, Uncle Moto. I see you have your new phone. Have you got any selfies on it?

Uncle Motohiro: Selfies? What are those?

Aki: Seriously? They're photos you take of yourself on your phone.

Uncle Motohiro: What? How do you do that?

Aki: _____ , you have to open the camera app on your phone. _____ is to press the little button with the arrows on it. That will turn the camera on you.

Uncle Motohiro: OK, then what?

Aki: It's selfie time! Stretch your arm out in front of you as far as you can. _____ point the lens at your face. Hold your face at an angle – it's more interesting that way. _____ , hit the button to take your photo!

Uncle Motohiro: Ugh! It's terrible!

Aki: Ha! That's what the delete button is for!

3 **Work in pairs.** Take turns spinning the wheel and explaining processes.

4 **Work in groups.** Think of three things you typically do in a week that can be explained as processes, such as making your lunch or getting ready for school. Explain these processes. Do your group members do these things in the same way?

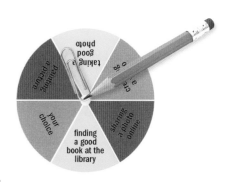

Go to page 169.

SPEAKING **115**

GRAMMAR ⌒091

Past passive: Describing past actions and processes

Goya created many of his works at night, by the light of a hat that had candles on it.

Many of Goya's works **were created** at night, by the light of a hat that had candles on it.

Painters explored many different styles.

Many different styles **were explored** by painters.

Artists usually made paint by mixing colours with oils.

Paint **was** usually **made** by mixing colours with oils.

1 **Listen.** Learn about portraits and the stories they tell. Then circle the verbs that you hear used in the past passive. ⌒092

ask	capture	create	die	display	do	invent
make	pay	require	spend	take	use	work

2 **Work in pairs.** Use the words to ask and answer questions in the past passive.

> Who painted the *Mona Lisa*?

> The *Mona Lisa* was painted by Leonardo da Vinci.

1. *Mona Lisa* / paint / da Vinci
2. Flyer III / build / Wright brothers
3. early camera / invent / Daguerre
4. cave paintings / create / early humans

Mona Lisa (La Gioconda)
by Leonardo da Vinci

3 **Work in pairs.** Look at *Portrait of a Young Woman*. Then answer questions using the past passive.

1. Who painted the portrait? _____

_____

2. What was worn by the subject? _____

_____

3. What do you think the subject was asked to do by the painter?

_____

_____

Portrait of a Young Woman
by Jean-Étienne Liotard

4 LEARN NEW WORDS Listen to learn more about painting. Then listen and repeat.
🎧 093 094

A **landscape** painting shows a scene from nature.

Although their subjects are often simple, still-life paintings can be **masterpieces**.

Some portraits aren't **realistic**. They're **abstract**.

5 Discuss in groups.

1. Do you prefer realistic or abstract paintings? Why?

2. Can landscapes and still-life paintings be abstract? Why or why not?

3. Discuss two works of art you consider masterpieces.

6 **Work independently.** Use the past passive to describe how you think one of the works of art on these pages was created. Write at least four sentences.

_____

_____

_____

_____

BRINGING STORIES TO LIFE

Do you love playing video games with really cool graphics? Or watching action films with amazing special effects? Thanks to advances in digital technology, modern animation can create detailed, lifelike images that move around the screen at incredible speeds. We experience animation in so many different forms, from the cartoons on our TVs to the emojis on our smartphones. But animation is nothing new. In fact, people have been trying to bring images to life for hundreds of years.

The earliest animation began in the 17th century with a device called the magic lantern. In the 19th century, other devices were developed that created movement when viewers spun them. By the turn of the

1650s

The magic lantern uses the light of a candle and painted pieces of glass to create moving images projected onto a wall. It becomes more sophisticated over time.

1832

The *phenakistoscope* is considered by many to have created the first true animation. To watch the animation, the viewer holds up a mirror and spins two illustrated disks. The spinning motion makes the illustrations seem to move.

1834

The *zoetrope* also uses a spinning motion to create animation. It quickly becomes more popular than the phenakistoscope because more than one person can watch at a time.

1891

American inventor Thomas Edison creates the *kinetoscope*. Viewers must look into the machine to watch a cartoon, which lasts about 13 seconds and contains around 50 images.

---

1 BEFORE YOU READ **Discuss in pairs.**

Which animated TV programmes and films did you watch as a child?

2 LEARN NEW WORDS **Find these words in the reading.** What do you think they mean? Use a thesaurus to find synonyms for each word. Then listen and repeat. ⌒095

animation	cartoon	illustrator
method	sophisticated	

3 WHILE YOU READ **Underline each of the different methods of animation mentioned in the text.** ⌒096

HOW ANIMATION HAS CHANGED OVER THE YEARS

20th century, artists around the world were developing short animated films using hand-drawn animation. Illustrators would create thousands of drawings for a single cartoon!

Throughout the 20th century, animators continued to develop different methods, from drawings to using clay figures. By the 1980s, digital animation was being developed. It quickly replaced traditional methods because it allowed cartoons to be produced in less time and with less money. Today, advanced digital animation methods aren't just used in cartoons and video games, but also to create special effects in live-action films. Animation has become so sophisticated that sometimes we can't distinguish it from reality!

1917

Argentine animator Quirino Cristiani creates the first animated film, *El Apóstol*. The film has 58,000 illustrations and is 70 minutes long.

1928

Mickey Mouse is born. Walt Disney changes animation forever by adding sound. *Steamboat Willie* was the first cartoon in which viewers could hear what was happening.

1980s – present

Digital animation is first developed in the 1980s. Today, sophisticated 3D animation is used for cartoons, video games and even live-action films.

4 AFTER YOU READ **Work in pairs to answer the questions.**

1. How was animation created with a magic lantern?
2. Name two differences between a phenakistoscope and a zoetrope.
3. How many drawings did Quirino Cristiani use to create the first animated film? How long was it?
4. How did Walt Disney's *Steamboat Willie* cartoon change animation?
5. Why did digital animation replace traditional methods?
6. What are two ways that 3D animation is used today?

5 **Work in pairs.** Compare the words and phrases you underlined with your partner. Then summarise how each method was used to tell a visual story.

6 **Discuss in groups.**

1. If you had to animate a story, which method would you choose? Why?
2. Go online to watch *Steamboat Willie*. Describe the cartoon in your own words. Compare it with cartoons that children watch today.

VIDEO ▶

1 BEFORE YOU WATCH Discuss in pairs. In the reading, you learnt that most modern animation is digital. How do you think digital animation is made? Describe the process.

2 Read. You're going to watch a video called *Animation Creation*. Look at the storyboard on this page and read the three sentences. Which idea do you think will be most related to the video's content? Circle the letter.

a. An animation is created more quickly than a live TV programme because there's little to prepare.

b. Animations are popular because they're easy to make and cost very little money.

c. Creating animations is a process that requires careful planning and decision-making.

3 WHILE YOU WATCH Create a flowchart showing the steps for creating an animation. Watch scene 7.1.

4 AFTER YOU WATCH Work in pairs to answer the questions.

1. Who are the people involved in making the animation?
2. What is the purpose of a mood board?
3. What are the three stages of creating an animation?
4. What is added at the animatic stage?
5. What is the last step in creating an animation?

A storyboard

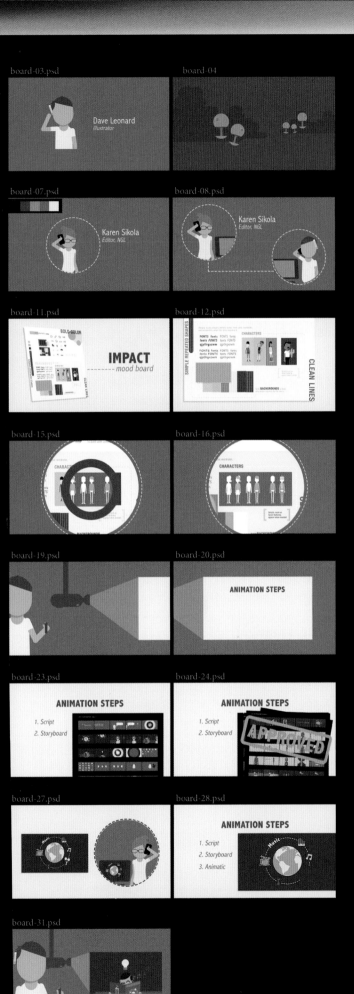

5 **Work in pairs.** In the video, the editor gives suggestions to the illustrator. What does she suggest? Tick the boxes. Then discuss how each suggestion would be helpful.

☐ Rewrite the script.

☐ Use cooler colours.

☐ Change the style of the characters.

☐ Design three different storyboards.

☐ Change the music.

6 **Work in pairs.** Compare the steps you created in your flowchart from Activity 3. Talk about what happens at each step. Do you think this happens with all of the animations you watch? Explain.

7 **YOU DECIDE** **Choose an activity.**

1. **Work independently.** Imagine you're a TV producer who's looking for an illustrator to create animations for a programme. Write an advertisement for the job. Explain what personality traits the illustrator needs. Describe the type of work the job requires.

2. **Work in pairs.** Find an animated video online and watch it without the audio. Create a new script and choose music for the video. Then play the video for the class, using your own narration and music.

3. **Work in groups.** Research a live TV programme you like and find out how it's produced. Create a Venn diagram to compare the process with the production of an animation. Present your comparison to the class.

Reported speech: Describing what others say

'I will save my money for art supplies because I'm learning to draw manga.'	She **says she will** save her money for art supplies because **she's learning** to draw manga. She **said she would** save her money for art supplies because **she was learning** to draw manga.
'Plan your ideas first.'	The teacher **tells/is telling/told** them **to plan** their ideas first.
'Can I borrow your pencil?'	He **asked if he could** borrow my pencil. He asked **to borrow** my pencil.

1 Listen. You will hear how to draw a manga. After you listen, circle the word to correctly complete the sentences. 🎧098

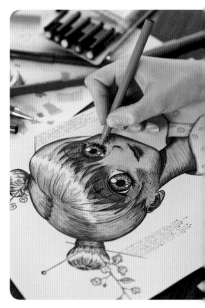

1. The speaker says that you first *have* / *had* to plan.
2. He tells us *to choose* / *chose* a story.
3. He said that the next step *is* / *was* to create a storyboard.
4. He tells us *not to worry* / *don't worry* about creating a perfect storyboard.
5. He told us we *can* / *could* scan the drawing, but that we *will* / *would* need special software to edit the work.
6. Then he asked us what we *think* / *thought*.

2 Work in pairs. Listen to the audio again. Then answer the questions using reported speech. 🎧099

1. What did the speaker tell us about the process of making a manga?

   He told us it took a lot of time.

2. What did he say about creating characters?

   _____

3. What did he tell us to do after the storyboard is complete?

   _____

4. What did the speaker ask us at the end?

   _____

3 Work in large groups. Cut out the cards and use them to play 'Telephone'. Use reported speech.

She told me to use quality pencils and pens for drawing.

'Use quality pencils and pens for drawing.'

Go to page 171.

WRITING

When we write stories, we often tell what others say. To do this, we can use reported speech. We can also surround the person's statement or question with quotation marks. Look at the following examples:

Annie asked if I was going to eat the apple.

'Are you going to eat the apple?' asked Annie.

Gil says it's a wonderful idea.

'It's a wonderful idea,' says Gil.

1 **Read the model.** Notice how the writer quotes people in the story. Underline examples.

Whenever I look at this photo, I think of an afternoon fishing with my grandfather. My grandfather loves fishing. When we were younger, he tried to get my brother and me excited about it. 'It's a wonderful way to spend the afternoon together,' he told us. Every Saturday he asked us to go with him. At first we would, but fishing seemed so boring to us. Eventually, we told him that fishing wasn't our thing. After that, he would go alone.

One Saturday afternoon not long ago, I changed my mind and decided to go with him. I thought that maybe I would enjoy fishing more now that a few years have passed. So down to the water we went. We got in the water, threw the line and waited. And waited. After three hours all we had was a single tiny fish.

'Grandpa, why do you like standing out here for hours like this?' I asked. 'You've done nothing all afternoon!'

'Well,' he said. 'When I was a boy, fishing wasn't "nothing". In fact, it was everything. I didn't have TV, or video games or smartphones. So I fished. Now, when I fish, I go back to being that boy. It was a happy time.'

This photo really changed how I see my grandfather. I don't just see a quiet older man, but rather somebody who has seen many changes and has had many experiences. Looking at the photo also reminds me that my opinion of fishing changed that afternoon. Straight after I took the picture, Grandpa felt a strong pull on his line. In an instant, the two of us were struggling to bring in the biggest fish I had ever seen! It was really exciting. From then on, I went fishing with him whenever I could.

2 **Work in pairs.** What story does the photo tell? How does the photo change the writer?

3 **Write.** Choose a photo of a friend or family member. Write the story your photo tells. Use reported speech and quotations to tell what people said.

NATIONAL GEOGRAPHIC

Tell Stories

'It's about getting close to people, listening and looking intimately at life and the world we live in. It's about telling meaningful stories that will create awareness and hopefully inspire change for the better.'

Ami Vitale
National Geographic Photographer

1. Watch scene 7.2.

2. Ami Vitale uses photography to tell other people's stories. What are some ways you can find out about people's stories? How can you tell them?

3. Think of a time when someone's life changed because another person told his/her story. Summarise what happened. Then discuss why people need to tell one another's stories.

Make an Impact

YOU DECIDE Choose a project.

1 **Create a flipbook.**

· Assemble a small book. Draw on each of the pages to create animation when you flip it.

· Share your book with the class. Describe the story it tells.

· Explain the process of making your book. Answer your classmates' questions.

2 **Profile a visual storyteller.**

· Go online to research visual storytellers. Select one to profile.

· Create a computer presentation about the person's life and work. Show examples of visual stories this person has told.

· Present your work to the class.

3 **Tell your own visual story.**

· Think of a cause or person that is important to you. Think of the story you want to tell about this subject.

· Choose a format for your story. You might choose to draw, paint, animate or use photographs.

· Create your visual story and share it with the class.

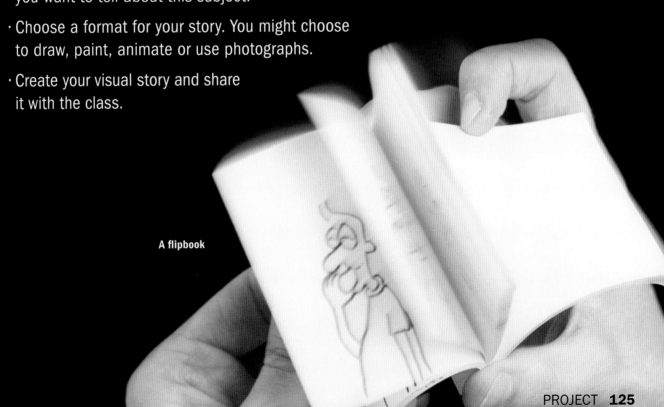

A flipbook

Unit 8
Perform and Create

'I like to think of music not just as music,
but as information.'
   Paul D. Miller, aka DJ Spooky

126

A performer breakdancing in a
cloud of coloured smoke

TO START

1. You've learnt about art forms such as painting,
   photography and animation. What are other ways
   people express themselves artistically?

2. DJ Spooky says that for him music is information. Do
   you agree with him? What do you learn from music?

3. What are some ways you like to express yourself?

1 **How important is music in your life? Why?**
Discuss. Then listen and read. 🎧 100

Music is an essential part of many people's lives. Whether it's live or recorded, music is a **means** of **entertainment** to almost everyone. But for musicians, music is about more than just enjoyment: it's a form of **self-expression**. When we think of creating music, we think of the **composers** who write music and **lyrics** and the **performers** who play these songs. But a different kind of musical self-expression has become popular over the last few decades: being a DJ. A DJ chooses and plays pre-recorded music for an audience. He or she mixes and **manipulates** the rhythms and **beats** using different creative methods. Although the style **varies** depending on the DJ, the result is usually a high-energy sound that's perfect for dancing.

The term *DJ* comes from the words *disc* and *jockey*. The word *disc* refers to a vinyl record. Records may seem old-fashioned to people who download music from the Internet, but many DJs today still use them to spin. At a club a DJ might mix on a computer, a tablet, a turntable or any combination of the three.

DJs don't just work at clubs. They play at events, such as weddings and birthday parties. DJs also play and discuss music on a podcast or at a radio station. In fact, DJs have been on the radio for more than a century. The very first DJ, Ray Newby, was only 16 when he played music on a small radio in 1909. Over the years, radio DJs chose what music to **expose** audiences to. Hearing their own songs on the radio brought musicians **satisfaction**. More importantly, a DJ playing your song was an indication that **fame** was on the way!

Today, DJs themselves are international stars. For example, Dutch-born DJ Tiësto **gained recognition** performing at the 2004 Summer Olympics. By 2012, he was earning millions of dollars a year. Some DJs use their fame to be **influential**. For example, DJ Spooky composed the *Terra Nova/Sinfonia Antarctica* to raise awareness about environmental issues. This is not your typical symphony. This music mix is the portrait of a continent threatened by climate change. For DJ Spooky, being a DJ is more than just playing music – it's about making others think!

A DJ spinning music on a turntable

2 **LEARN NEW WORDS** Listen and repeat. ∩ 101

3 **Work in pairs.** Are DJs popular in your country? Have you listened to or seen a DJ perform? What's it like?

4 **Read and write the words from the list.** Make any necessary changes.

beat	composer	entertainment	influential	lyrics
manipulate	means	performer	satisfaction	vary

Paul D. Miller is a musician, writer and _____ who performs as DJ Spooky. He's known around the world for his ability to entertain audiences by mixing hip-hop _____ . But DJ Spooky sees his complex work as much more than _____ . He sees it as a _____ of informing the public about important issues such as climate change, sustainability and the role of technology in society. He wants his music to be _____ in changing how people think.

DJ Spooky's multimedia presentations _____ from recordings, animation, books and videos to lectures and art installations. He even has a free, open-source app that provides other DJs with tools to mix, scratch and add electronic effects to their own music. This way they can be _____ , too.

DJ Spooky

5 **LEARN NEW WORDS Listen to these words and match them to the definitions.** Then listen and repeat. 🎧 **102** **103**

enjoyment	essential	indication	symphony

_____ 1. happiness or pleasure

_____ 2. necessary

_____ 3. a musical composition with many instruments

_____ 4. a sign or signal

6 **YOU DECIDE Choose an activity.**

1. **Work independently.** Think of a DJ performance you've seen, or find one online. Write a review of the performance.

2. **Work in pairs.** Discuss the following questions: Why is music important? Where and how do you listen to music? Where do you get information about new music?

3. **Work in groups.** Research a popular DJ, and find a sample of his or her recordings. Present your research to the class. Play the audio clip and describe the music. Talk about the DJ's style and message.

SPEAKING STRATEGY 🎧 104

Asking for feelings and opinions	Expressing feelings and opinions
How do you feel about <u>jazz</u>? What are your thoughts on <u>hip-hop</u>?	I'm crazy about <u>jazz</u>. I'm a big fan of <u>hip-hop</u>. It's all right, I guess. I'm not wild about <u>hip-hop</u>.
What do you think about <u>going to the opera</u>?	I can't stand <u>listening to opera</u>.

1 **Listen.** How do the speakers ask for and express opinions? Write the phrases you hear. 🎧 105

2 **Read and complete the dialogue.**

Abram: Marina, do you play an instrument?

Marina: Yes, I actually play three. _____ music!

Abram: Me, too. _____ playing the guitar. It's how I express myself. What instruments do you play?

Marina: Well, I've been playing piano since I was four. _____ It's not my favourite. I play the violin and the flute, too. The violin is my favourite.

Abram: Yeah, string instruments are great because you can play them anywhere. I tried to play the piano, but _____ being stuck in the house all day practising. With my guitar I can practise wherever I go.

Marina: _____ getting together to do a song – me on the violin, you on the guitar?

Abram: Sure! We'd have to think about what musical style we'd want to work on.

Marina: _____ rock? I know some really cool songs with violin solos.

Abram: Sounds great!

3 **Work in groups.** Take turns. Use a coin to move (heads = 1 space; tails = 2 spaces). Express your feelings and opinions.

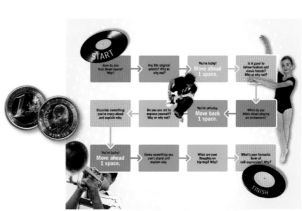

4 **Work in pairs.** Find out what you have in common. Find three things that you're both crazy about and three things you can't stand.

Go to page 173.

GRAMMAR 🎧 106

Gerunds and infinitives

Dancing is a popular form of self-expression.

Some people like **performing/to perform** as comedians.

Other people are interested in **acting** in videos and plays.

Building an audience of fans for a performer's work is important.

It's important **to build** an audience of fans for a performer's work.

Post information about the show on social media **to get** a big audience.

A living statue

1 Read. Complete the sentences with forms of the verbs in brackets.

_____ (Express) yourself can happen in unusual ways. Some people are enthusiastic about _____ (pretend) to be statues or sculptures. They like _____ (trick) people! If the performers are outside, people usually walk by without _____ (realise) the statues are actually alive. Other living statues prefer _____ (work) as entertainers for companies that send them to different events and locations. And others like _____ (enter) contests. For instance, it's the dream of many living statues _____ (win) the annual International World Championship of Living Statues. _____ (Judge) takes place in three categories: professionals, amateurs and children.

2 Work in pairs. Rewrite the sentences.

1. Seeing a living statue move would surprise me.

   It _____

2. Creating an interesting look is important for a living statue.

   It _____

3. Standing still for a long time can be very difficult.

   It _____

3 Work in groups. Take turns creating and answering questions using the words provided with gerunds or infinitives.

> Do you ever get bored with dancing?

> No, but I get bored with watching dance programmes on TV.

| bored with | excited about | like | prefer |

4 **LEARN NEW WORDS Listen to learn about dancing.** Then listen and repeat. 🎧 107 108

A **choreographer** first plans out how a group of **ballet** dancers will dance, deciding when and how they move with the music. Then the dancers practise this dance during **rehearsal**.

Folk dancing

5 **Read.** Match the term to its clue.

_____ 1. folk dancing   a. a dance typically performed to classical music

_____ 2. choreographer   b. dancing to fast, rhythmic music

_____ 3. hip-hop dancing   c. performing a dance that's been done for generations

_____ 4. ballet   d. a time for working with a choreographer or director

_____ 5. rehearsal   e. a person who plans dancers' movements

6 **Work in groups.** Talk about different forms of artistic expression. Use words from each box, plus a gerund or infinitive.

animation	be essential
dance	dislike
DJ	interested in
living statue	know about
music composition	prefer
paint	

> I'm interested in working as a DJ. What do you think?

> Well, it's essential to know a lot about music! Do you?

MUSIC FOR CHILLING OUT

1. **BEFORE YOU READ Discuss in pairs.** Look at the photo. Describe what you see.

2. **LEARN NEW WORDS Find the words below in the reading.** What do you think they mean? Find antonyms for the words *freeze* and *dirty*. Then listen and repeat. 🎧 109

   | melt | orchestra | pure | stage | tribute |

3. **WHILE YOU READ Draw two conclusions about the Ice Music Festival.** 🎧 110

4. **AFTER YOU READ Work in pairs to answer the questions.**

   1. Who is Terje Isungset?
   2. What does Terje refer to as 'art by accident'?
   3. Who works together to make the instruments?
   4. How are the instruments created?
   5. What are three challenges facing musicians who perform at the festival?

5. **Work in pairs.** Compare the conclusions that you drew in Activity 3 with your partner's. Think of an additional conclusion you can draw about the festival.

6. **Discuss in groups.**

   1. The performers at the Ice Music Festival must make music with their instruments with little rehearsal. What are the disadvantages of this process? What might the benefits be?
   2. Describe a concert or music festival that you attended. What do you think organisers did to plan the event? Compare the process with that of the Ice Music Festival.
   3. Would you like to attend the Ice Music Festival? Why or why not?

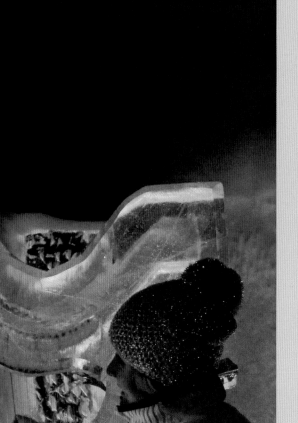

You've never heard music *this* cool!

Winters in Norway can be long and dark, with very little sunlight. But winter can be one of the most exciting times to visit, especially for music lovers. The annual Ice Music Festival celebrates the sounds of winter. At the festival, held in the small mountain town of Geilo, world-class musicians play frozen instruments in an orchestra unlike any other.

The first Ice Music Festival took place in 2006, but its director, Terje Isungset, had been making instruments from ice since 1999. An innovative musician known for using natural elements in his instruments, Terje described discovering the capability to create sound with ice as 'art by accident'. Once he learnt of the different sounds produced with ice, he began experimenting with a variety of instruments, including harps, horns and xylophones. In 2005, he launched All Ice Records, a record label for ice-only music.

It's the instruments that make the Ice Music Festival unique. The process of creating them begins at a lake about 40 km. (25 mi.) from Geilo. Here the ice is clean and pure, perfect for making music. The ice must be natural. Man-made ice does not produce the same sound. Workers cut 272 kg. (600 lb.) blocks of ice from the lake and transport them back to town on snowmobiles. Next, ice sculptor Bill Covitz works alongside the musicians for hours to create instruments. Bill carves individual parts of each instrument, then uses water as glue to hold the parts together.

Working with ice creates new challenges for the musicians. The ice instruments are much more fragile than regular instruments. And performers can't play familiar songs because they don't know what sounds the ice instruments will make. 'You cannot go on stage and expect a certain sound. You have to play with the sound that instrument actually can make. And then try to create good music out of this,' says Terje. Perhaps the biggest challenge, though, is being sure that the instruments don't melt! The musicians' body heat is a threat to the instruments, especially for horn players who are blowing warm air right into the ice!

Despite the challenges, the festival brings people from around the world to hear this incredible tribute to winter, nature and music.

A musician plays a harp made from ice.

1 **BEFORE YOU WATCH Discuss in pairs.** You're going to watch a video about *stage fright*. Based on each of the words in the phrase, what do you think stage fright is? Who do you think would have stage fright?

2 **Read and tick.** The video you're going to watch is called *Stage Fright in the Spotlight*. Based on the title, predict what you'll learn. Tick all that apply.

☐ What stage fright is
☐ Why it's unusual to have stage fright
☐ What happens when you suffer from stage fright
☐ How to handle stage fright
☐ Why you should be afraid to be onstage

3 **WHILE YOU WATCH List two ways to handle stage fright.** Watch scene 8.1.

4 **AFTER YOU WATCH Work in pairs to decide if each sentence is *true* or *false*.** Tick the correct answer.

1. When you suffer from stage fright, your heart might beat faster. **T** **F**
2. Few people suffer from stage fright. **T** **F**
3. In a survey, the only thing people fear more than talking in front of others is death. **T** **F**
4. Entertainers may suffer from stage fright. **T** **F**
5. Understanding why stage fright happens is important for dealing with it. **T** **F**
6. Imagining the audience clapping and cheering will make you more afraid. **T** **F**

5 **Work in pairs.** Think about your answer for Activity 1. Were you correct? Do you ever suffer from stage fright? If so, when? Explain what happens to you when you have to talk or perform in front of others. If not, explain how you handle speaking or performing in front of others.

6 **Discuss in groups.**

1. What do you fear most: flying, heights or speaking in front of other people? Explain your answer.

2. Talk about a time when you had to perform alone on a stage. When was it? How did you feel?

3. Think of at least two additional ways to deal with stage fright.

7 **YOU DECIDE** **Choose an activity.**

1. **Work independently.** Imagine you went to a performance in which the performer froze with stage fright. Write a review of the performance, including advice for the performer's next show.

2. **Work in pairs.** Role-play a dialogue between a performer and a choreographer or other trainer at a rehearsal. The performer is nervous that he will get stage fright during the performance. The trainer offers advice on what to do.

3. **Work in groups.** Find a video online of a performance where someone suffered from stage fright. Show the video to the class. Explain what happened and what the performer could have done differently.

GRAMMAR 🎧 111

Sense verbs + infinitive: Describing what you see, hear and feel

Did you **see the band perform** in concert?

No, but I **heard them sing** on the radio.

Come on! Let's **watch the DJ spin** records.

We'd **been hearing them practise** for days before their performance.

1 **Listen.** Write sentences in the table about what the people did. 🎧 112

	See	Hear	Feel	Watch
Jian	He saw the WagakkiBand play.			
Mei				

2 **Work independently.** Write sentences about your own experiences using the verbs below.

1. hear / play   *I've never heard the WagakkiBand play before.*

2. see / dance _____

3. feel / move _____

4. watch / juggle _____

3 **Work in pairs.** Cut out the cards and take turns selecting one. Then discuss your own experiences.

I've only ever seen an opera singer perform once. What about you?

I saw an opera singer perform on TV.

See an opera singer perform

Go to page 175.

WRITING

When we write an explanatory essay, we want to teach our reader about a topic. We must identify the topic in the first paragraph. Then we must provide additional facts, details and examples to help the reader better understand the topic. An explanatory essay does not include the writer's opinion.

1 **Read the model.** The writer is teaching us about a type of puppet show. Cross out the two sentences that don't belong in the explanatory essay.

Thai puppet performances are a unique form of cultural expression. I saw a Thai puppet show and it was amazing! In a performance, three puppeteers work together to move one beautiful, lifelike puppet to traditional music. Puppeteers must know Thai classical dance. As they dance, each puppeteer holds a wooden rod with a string attached to control different parts of the puppet.

There were different sizes and types of puppets used in Thai puppet performances throughout history, but the puppets used in modern performances are about 60 cm. (2 ft.) high and made of bamboo. Their heads are very realistic, and they wear detailed, elegant costumes. In fact, the costumes are often decorated with gold and jewels. On the inside, puppets have around 16 strings that connect their body parts to one another. Moving these strings allows the puppets to move smoothly and naturally.

Puppets have been a form of entertainment in Thailand for around 300 years, but the traditional Thai puppet performances gained popularity in the early 20th century. Master puppeteer Krae Saptawanit, who first created the small puppet in 1901, travelled around the country doing performances. However, interest in the shows decreased in the mid-20th century after Saptawanit's death. In 1985, a group of puppeteers formed to reintroduce the traditional art. I think this group is really good – probably better at performing the shows than the original artists. Today, these puppet shows are popular with local people and tourists alike.

2 **Work in pairs.** What did you learn about the art of Thai puppetry? Would you like to see a performance? Why or why not?

3 **Write.** Write an essay to explain a type of artistic expression. Remember to provide facts, details and examples to teach your reader about the topic.

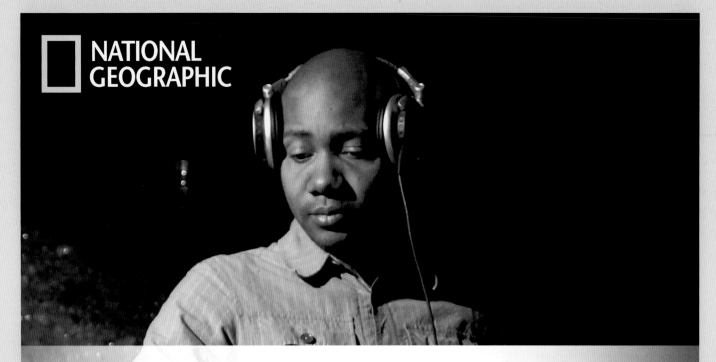

Do Your Own Thing

'There are so many people who just let the world define them. What happens when you begin to realise another world is possible – that's art.'

Paul D. Miller, aka DJ Spooky

National Geographic Explorer, Artist/Writer/Musician

1. **Watch scene 8.2.**

2. What would you say your 'own thing' is? How does it bring you closer to other people? How does it help you stand out?

3. Do you let the world define you? Or do you define who you are? Or both? Explain with examples.

Make an Impact

YOU DECIDE Choose a project.

1 Perform for your class.

- Choose a type of performing art to perform for the class.

- Before you perform, explain what you're going to do. Give background on the history and popularity of your performing art form. Talk about what you need to know and have in order to perform.

- Hold a question-and-answer session with the class after your performance.

2 Interview a performer.

- Think of a performing artist in your community. Prepare ten questions to ask the artist about the type of work he or she does.

- Conduct your interview. Audio record or film it.

- Play your interview for the class.

3 Make a timeline.

- Choose a type of performing art. Research its history.

- Make a timeline to illustrate the history of this performing art. Use photos to show how it's changed.

- Present your timeline to the class.

Express Yourself

NOT Your Typical Performance

Make up

Costumes

A visual story

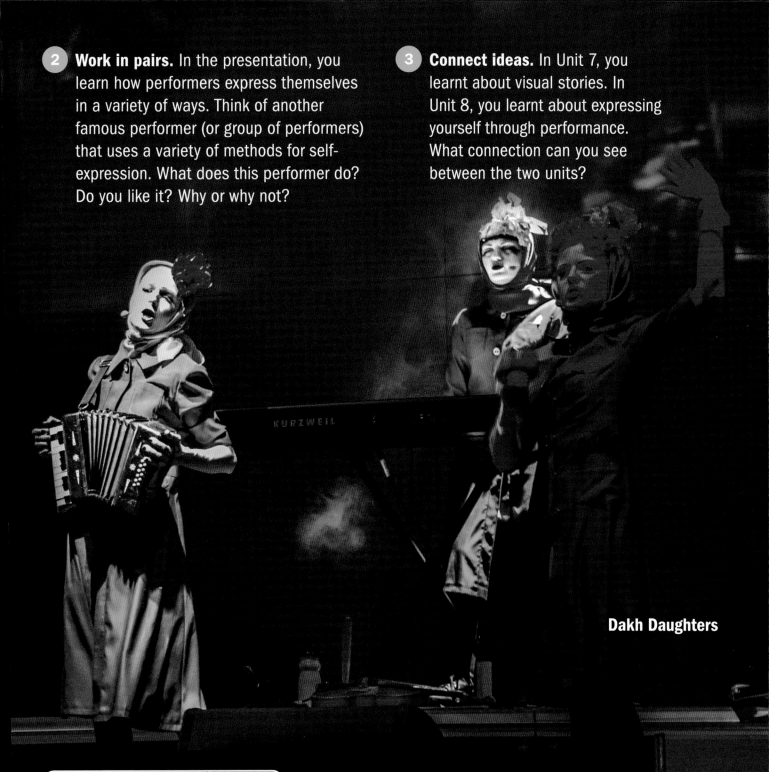

2 **Work in pairs.** In the presentation, you learn how performers express themselves in a variety of ways. Think of another famous performer (or group of performers) that uses a variety of methods for self-expression. What does this performer do? Do you like it? Why or why not?

3 **Connect ideas.** In Unit 7, you learnt about visual stories. In Unit 8, you learnt about expressing yourself through performance. What connection can you see between the two units?

Dakh Daughters

A variety of instruments

4 **YOU DECIDE** **Choose an activity.**

1. Choose a topic:
   - visual stories
   - performances

2. Choose a way to express yourself:
   - a storyboard or animation
   - a computer presentation
   - a performance

3. Present your work.

Unit 5
Past perfect

1 **Listen.** Notice how *had* sounds in the past perfect. 🎧 123

A: Had anyone tried to fly before the Wright brothers?

B: Yes, I think flying had been attempted by many people.

A: Until the lesson, Tim had never realised that bats are mammals.

B: I hadn't either!

When *had* comes after the subject or a question word, the pronunciation is often contracted *'d* or reduced.

The word *had* is not reduced when it comes at the beginning of a question, in a negative statement or in a short answer. The vowel sound is clearly pronounced.

2 **Listen and repeat.** Circle the two reduced examples of *had*. 🎧 124

1. A: Who had never seen a bat up close?
    B: I hadn't. They're so small!
2. Cindy had always wanted to learn about birds.
3. A: Had you seen a bat before, Matt?
    B: Yes, I had. But I hadn't realised they were mammals.

3 **Work in pairs.** Listen and complete the conversation with *had* or *hadn't*. Circle each reduced *had*. Then practise the conversation. 🎧 125

A. Some ancient bird fossils are missing. The guard _____ (had) just finished his breakfast when he heard something downstairs. But all he found was the case open and the fossils missing.

B: _____ anyone signed in?

A: No, no one _____ signed in, but someone _____ been in there.

B: OK, talk to anyone who might've seen something.

A: Yes. We will. One student _____ been studying near the door at the time, but says he _____ been paying attention.

Unit 6
Final *d* + *you*

1 **Listen.** Notice how the final *d* links with the *y* in *you*. 🎧 126

Would you go to Mars?
⌣
j

Could you help me with my essay?
⌣
j

Did you know that Mars had water?
⌣
j

Who told you about Space Camp?
⌣
j

When the final *d* links with the *y*, it forms a *j* sound (as in **j**uice).

2 **Listen and repeat.** Draw an arrow to link the final *d* words to *you*. 🎧 127

1. Where did you go on your last holiday?
2. If you could, would you go to the moon?
3. Who called you or texted you last week?
4. Did you get a good mark on your last test?
5. What did you do last weekend?

3 **Work in pairs.** Take turns asking and answering the questions in Activity 2. Make sure you link the *d* and *y* sounds.

> Where did you go on your last holiday?

> I went to the mountains with my family.

> What did you do there?

> We went skiing.

Unit 7

Final /ə/ sound

1 **Listen.** Listen for the final ə sounds. Can you hear them? ⌒ **128**

Ami Vitale is a photographer.

The painter asked if he could paint her portrait.

She told him she wanted to be an inventor.

Many professions end with the ə sound. Sometimes this is spelt *-er*, and sometimes it's spelt *-or*.

2 **Work in pairs.** Listen to the names of the professions. Decide if they end in *-er* or *-or*. ⌒ **129**

1. philosoph _____ .
2. art direct _____ .
3. web develop _____ .
4. doct _____ .
5. carpent _____ .

3 **Write the names of the professions.** Then listen and check. ⌒ **130**

1. Someone who works in a school is a _____ .

2. The famous _____ played the part of Hamlet.

3. Jack Andraka is a young _____ .

4. Someone who studies the stars is an _____ .

Unit 8

Rhythm and stress

1 **Listen.** Notice the rhythm. ⌒ **131**

● ● ●
mu **si** cian

You **miss** him.

Stressed words or syllables create a strong beat. The rhythm of English depends on the number of strong beats, not the number of words. Listen to these sentences. The rhythm is the same for each.

●   ●   ●

Joe   **plays**   **drums**.

Joe can   **play** the **drums**.

Joe is   **play**ing the **drums**.

Joe has   been **play**ing the **drums**.

Joe should've been **play**ing the **drums**.

The unstressed words are often shortened to keep the rhythm.

2 **Listen and repeat sentences *a* and *b*.** Clap to the rhythm. Then listen to sentences 1–5 and match the rhythm pattern. Write *a* or *b*. ⌒ **132**

●   ●   ● ●
a. I'm **cra**zy about **jazz**.   b. I **can't stand op**era.

1. ___*a*___ Her **mu**sic is **great**.
2. _____ I **felt** the **ground shake**.
3. _____ Is he **go**ing to the **show**?
4. _____ I **saw** the **band play**.
5. _____ Her **voice** is **beau**tiful.

3 **Work in pairs.** Listen and repeat the dialogues. Then practise them, adding your ideas. Use correct rhythm. ⌒ **133**

I can **play** a **mu**sical **in**strument.

The gui**tar**.

What instrument?

1. A: I can **play** a
   musical **in**strument.
   B: **What in**strument?

2. A: I **can't play** _____ .
   B: **That's** a **shame**.

3. A: I'm **cra**zy about
   this **band**.
   B: **What band** is it?

Irregular Verbs

Infinitive	Past simple	Past participle	Infinitive	Past simple	Past participle
be	were	been	leave	left	left
beat	beat	beaten	lend	lent	lent
become	became	become	let	let	let
begin	began	begun	lie (down)	lay	lain
bend	bent	bent	light	lit	lit
bet	bet	bet	lose	lost	lost
bite	bit	bitten	make	made	made
bleed	bled	bled	mean	meant	meant
blow	blew	blown	meet	met	met
break	broke	broken	overcome	overcame	overcome
bring	brought	brought	pay	paid	paid
build	built	built	put	put	put
burn	burnt	burnt	quit	quit	quit
buy	bought	bought	read	read	read
carry	carried	carried	ride	rode	ridden
catch	caught	caught	ring	rang	rung
choose	chose	chosen	rise	rose	risen
come	came	come	run	ran	run
cost	cost	cost	say	said	said
cut	cut	cut	see	saw	seen
deal	dealt	dealt	sell	sold	sold
dig	dug	dug	send	sent	sent
dive	dived	dived	set	set	set
do	did	done	sew	sewed	sewn
draw	drew	drawn	shake	shook	shaken
dream	dreamt	dreamt	shine	shone	shone
drink	drank	drunk	show	showed	shown
drive	drove	driven	shrink	shrank	shrunk
dry	dried	dried	shut	shut	shut
eat	ate	eaten	sing	sang	sung
fall	fell	fallen	sink	sank	sunk
feed	fed	fed	sit	sat	sat
feel	felt	felt	sleep	slept	slept
fight	fought	fought	slide	slid	slid
find	found	found	speak	spoke	spoken
flee	fled	fled	spend	spent	spent
fly	flew	flown	spin	spun	spun
forbid	forbade	forbidden	stand	stood	stood
forget	forgot	forgotten	steal	stole	stolen
forgive	forgave	forgiven	stick	stuck	stuck
freeze	froze	frozen	sting	stung	stung
fry	fried	fried	stink	stank	stunk
get	got	got	strike	struck	struck
give	gave	given	swear	swore	sworn
go	went	gone	sweep	swept	swept
grind	ground	ground	swim	swam	swum
grow	grew	grown	swing	swung	swung
hang	hung	hung	take	took	taken
have	had	had	teach	taught	taught
hear	heard	heard	tear	tore	torn
hide	hid	hidden	tell	told	told
hit	hit	hit	think	thought	thought
hold	held	held	throw	threw	thrown
hurt	hurt	hurt	understand	understood	understood
keep	kept	kept	wake	woke	woken
kneel	knelt	knelt	wear	wore	worn
knit	knitted	knitted	weave	wove	woven
know	knew	known	win	won	won
lay	laid	laid	write	wrote	written
lead	led	led			

Two-word verbs – Inseparable

Verb	Meaning	Sample sentence
amount to	be the same as; turn out to be	The total **amounts to** five hundred. Some people thought he would not **amount to** anything, but he became famous.
apply for	to make a request	Do you plan to **apply for** a summer job?
apply to	be relevant	The rules **apply to** everyone!
ask around	ask several people	I'll **ask around** in case anyone found a lost phone.
break down	stop functioning	The car **broke down** yesterday.
break up	end a relationship	Did you hear that Lara and Renato **broke up**?
calm down	relax after being angry	**Calm down**! Everything will be OK.
check in	register at a hotel or airport	We can't **check in** until one o'clock.
check out	leave a hotel	He **checked out** at 10.20 and went straight to the airport.
cheer up	become happier	**Cheer up**! I'm sure your team will do better next time.
come across	find unexpectedly	I **came across** a very interesting article about crocodiles.
come from	originate in	Mangoes originally **come from** Asia.
count on	rely on	Please be there on time. I'm **counting on** you!
dress up	wear nice clothes	Mum, do I really need to **dress up** for the party?
eat out	eat at a restaurant	Why don't we **eat out** on Friday?
end up	eventually do/decide	We **ended up** going to the cinema last night.
engage in	take part in	The head teacher **engaged in** talks with the student council.
fall apart	break into pieces	Mum, I need a new desk. This one's **falling apart**.
fall down	fall to the ground	The vase **fell down** and smashed.
find out	learn	I was so excited when I **found out** we were going to Spain!
fit in	blend in; belong because you're similar	Teenagers wear certain clothes to **fit in**.
get along	be friendly with someone	I really like Tom. We **get along** well.
get over	recover from a problem	I know she's upset you didn't call her, but she'll **get over** it.
get together	meet; gather	Let's **get together** on Wednesday after school!
get up	get out of bed; rise	I **get up** at seven o'clock every day.
give in	surrender; quit	I won't **give in** to pressure from my friends.
give up	stop trying	This puzzle is really hard, but we won't **give up**!
go ahead	do; begin to do	Why don't you **go ahead** and invite her to the party?
go back	return	He **went back** to the site and discovered a second dinosaur.
go over	review	Let's **go over** the presentation before the lesson.
grow up	become an adult	I **grew up** in China.
hang in	stay positive	**Hang in** there. I'm sure you'll find the phone.
hang on	wait	**Hang on** a minute. I'm on the phone.
hang out	spend time	Do you want to **hang out** on Saturday?
hold on	wait	**Hold on** a second! I think I found the answer.
lead to	cause to happen	His research **led to** the discovery of a new species.

Verb	Meaning	Sample sentence
light up	become bright	The sky **lit up** with fireworks.
log in/on	sign in to a website or app	I can't **log in** because I can't remember my password.
look after	take care of	I have to **look after** my little sister on Sunday.
look back	think about things that happened in the past	**Looking back**, I think the other project topic was more interesting.
look for	try to find	What are you **looking for**? Did you lose something?
look into	try to find out about	I need to **look into** it. I'll let you know tomorrow.
not care for	not like	I do**n't** really **care for** opera.
pass away	die	I heard Kim's grandma **passed away**.
prey on	hunt and kill for food	Do lions **prey on** zebras?
rave about	talk or write very enthusiastically	Critics are **raving about** the new film.
rely on	trust; depend on	Do you think we **rely on** technology too much?
run away	escape; leave	Our dog **ran away**!
run into	meet unexpectedly; collide	Yesterday I **ran into** my old teacher. I **ran into** a tree.
stand out	be noticeable	I was the only one wearing purple. I really **stood out**.
take off	start to fly	The flight **took off** on time.
turn out	result; happen	I thought everyone in my family had a mobile phone. It **turns out** my uncle refuses to get one!
wake up	stop sleeping	I usually **wake up** at six o'clock.
warm up	prepare for exercise	Do you **warm up** before football games?
work out	be successful; exercise	Everyone liked our presentation. It **worked out** well! I prefer to **work out** in the gym when it's cold.

Two-word verbs – Separable

Verb	Meaning	Sample sentence
back up	support	His friends **backed** him **up**.
call off	cancel	They had planned a party, but they had to **call** it **off**.
calm down	help relax	Let's play soft music to **calm** the baby **down**.
carry out	do or complete something	They are **carrying out** research on ancient birds.
check out	observe; notice	**Check out** my new phone!
cheer up	try to make someone happy	Why don't we get some flowers to **cheer** her **up**?
clean up	organise; clean	Can you **clean** that **up**? Guests are arriving soon.
cut down	make something fall to the ground	They're **cutting down** too many trees.
cut off	remove by cutting	Did you read about that hiker that had to **cut off** his own arm?
draw in	capture the interest	This book really **drew** me **in**.
equip with	supply with	They **equipped** the astronauts **with** extra oxygen tanks.
fill out/in	write information in a form	Remember to **fill out** the form before the end of the week. **Fill in** your details on page 6.

Verb	Meaning	Sample sentence
fill up	fill to the top	Don't **fill up** the cup. I need room for milk.
find out	discover information	How did you **find** that **out**?
get across	make understandable	We need to add more examples to **get** the idea **across**!
give back	return something	Have you still got my book? Can you **give** it **back** to me?
give up	stop (a habit)	I'm **giving up** coffee!
hand in	submit	Did you **hand in** your homework on time?
hand out	distribute	I'll make copies and **hand** them **out**.
let down	disappoint	I really want you to come to the party. Don't **let me down**.
let in	allow to come in	They didn't **let** him **in** with his rucksack.
light up	make bright	At night the stars **light** the sky **up**.
look up	find information	Can you **look** it **up** in a dictionary?
make up	lie about; invent	That can't be true. I think he **made** it **up**.
mix up	confuse things or people	They always **mix** me **up** with my sister.
put off	postpone	Can we **put off** the meeting until next week?
put together	assemble	Can you help me **put** this **together**?
take down	remove	They **took down** the painting because it was controversial.
take off	remove	**Take off** that coat. You'll be too hot.
take over	gain control of	He **took over** the company when his father died.
throw away	put in the rubbish; get rid of	Don't **throw away** plastic bottles. Recycle them.
track down	find after a long search	I'm trying to **track down** a friend from my childhood.
try on	put on to see if it fits	I **tried on** my sister's shoes, but they didn't fit.
turn away	reject; refuse to admit	Hundreds of people were **turned away** from the audition.
turn down	decrease the strength	**Turn** the TV **down** a bit. It's too loud.
turn off	power off	Don't forget to **turn off** the lights when you leave.
turn on	power on	**Turn on** the TV. The match has started!
turn up	increase the strength	I can't hear. Can you **turn up** the volume?
warm up	make warmer	Can you **warm up** the milk?
work out	find a solution	I'm sure you'll **work** it **out**.

Three-word verbs – Inseparable

Verb	Meaning	Sample sentence
add up to	become a certain amount; result in something	The total **adds up to** two hundred.
break up with	end a relationship	She **broke up with** her boyfriend last week.
come down with	become ill	He **came down with** a cold.
come up against	face; confront	He **came up against** many obstacles during his research.
come up with	think of; find a solution	She **came up with** an excellent plan.
cut down on	use less of; do less	You should **cut down on** your screen time!
get along with	be friendly with	My sister **gets along with** everyone!
get round to	find time to finally do	I finally **got round to** writing my blog.
get away with	not get caught	How did you **get away with** not doing your homework?
get back into	become interested again	I stopped playing football two years ago, but then I **got back into** it.

Verb	Meaning	Sample sentence
get out of	avoid doing something you don't want to do	I think that's just an excuse to **get out of** doing the project!
give up on	lose hope that somebody or something will succeed	I **gave up on** trying to become an athlete.
grow out of	change your mind over time; become too big for	He wants to be a rock star, but I'm sure he'll **grow out of** it. You'll **grow out of** that jacket before winter is over!
look down on	feel that somebody is less important	Many people **looked down on** him and his art, but he went on to become a famous artist.
look forward to	be excited about (something in the future)	I **look forward to** going on holiday.
look out for	protect; take care of	He's very selfish! He only **looks out for** himself.
look up to	have a lot of respect for	Many youngsters **look up to** athletes or pop stars.
play around with	try several options	I **played around with** it until I found the problem!
put up with	tolerate	Our teacher doesn't **put up with** bad behaviour.
run out of	use everything	I think we've **run out of** milk. Can you get some?
stand up for	defend	Don't let him make fun of you. **Stand up for** yourself!
watch out for	be alert; anticipate	**Watch out for** deer crossing the road!

Verbs followed by infinitives and gerunds

Verbs followed by infinitive			Verbs followed by infinitive or noun/pronoun + infinitive		Verbs followed by noun/pronoun + infinitive	
He **agreed to go**.			He **wants to learn** French. I **want him to learn** French.		I **convinced her to try** sushi.	
afford	deserve	offer	ask	prepare	cause	motivate
agree	fail	plan	choose	promise	challenge	order
appear	happen	pretend	dare	want	convince	persuade
arrange	hesitate	refuse	expect	wish	empower	remind
attempt	hope	seem	need	would like	forbid	tell
care	intend	tend			force	urge
claim	learn	vow			hire	warn
decide	manage	wait			invite	
demand						

Verbs followed by gerund or noun/pronoun + infinitive		Verbs followed by a gerund				
They don't **allow surfing** here. They didn't **allow him to surf** here.		You should **avoid swimming** there.				
advise		admit	delay	imagine	mind	report
allow		anticipate	deny	involve	miss	resist
encourage		appreciate	discuss	justify	postpone	risk
permit		avoid	dislike	keep	practise	suggest
require		can't help	enjoy	look forward to	put off	understand
		carry on	feel like	mention	recommend	
		consider	finish			

Verbs followed by infinitive or gerund (similar meaning)			Verbs followed by infinitive or gerund (different meaning)	
I **hate waking** up early. I **hate to wake** up early.			I **remember going** there last year. I **remembered to go** to the shop.	
begin	hate	prefer	forget	remember
can't bear	like	propose	go on	stop
can't stand	love	start	quit	try
continue			regret	

Insects evolved from ancient animals that lived in water.

Argue YES or NO.

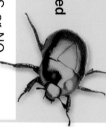

Pterosaurs were too big to generate powered flight, so they just glided.

Argue YES or NO.

Contagious behaviour such as yawning can sometimes cross species.

Argue YES or NO.

Hollow bones in pterosaurs and birds reduced weight and supported wings in flight.

Argue YES or NO.

Bats evolved from large dinosaurs that lived on the ground.

Argue YES or NO.

Over millions of years in the future, flight may eventually evolve in humans.

Argue YES or NO.

Flight evolved because it helped creatures find new sources of food and escape predators.

Argue YES or NO.

All birds that fly have got wings, but not all birds that have got wings fly.

Argue YES or NO.

Birth order is the best way to understand your personality.

Argue YES or NO.

Feathers appeared before flight and helped control body temperature.

Argue YES or NO.

Cockroaches are as careful about being clean as cats are.

Argue YES or NO.

Cotton plants need only small amounts of pesticides, water and energy to produce crops used in clothing.

Argue YES or NO.

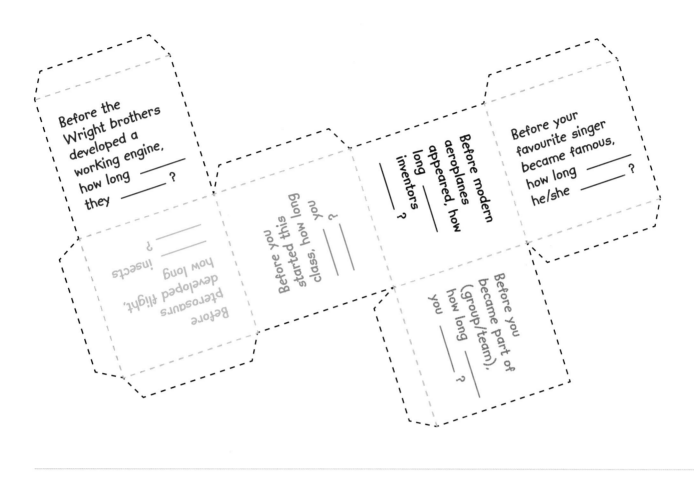

Before the Wright brothers developed a working engine, how long _____ they _____ ?

Before pterosaurs developed flight, how long insects _____ ?

Before you started this class, how long you _____ ?

Before modern aeroplanes appeared, how long inventors _____ ?

Before your favourite singer became famous, how long he/she _____ ?

Before you became part of (group/team), how long you _____ ?

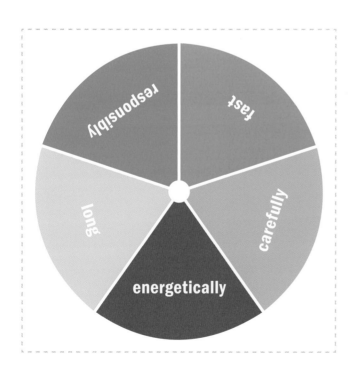

responsibly

fast

long

carefully

energetically

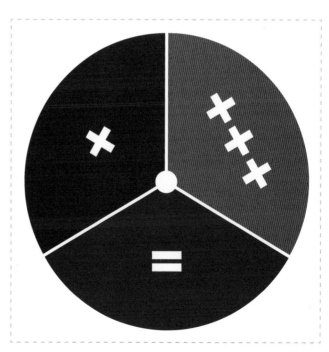

Water flowing
on Mars

The surface
of Mars, in the Valles
Marineris area

A sand dune
on Mars

An illustration
of a dust storm
on Mars

Round balls
of minerals found
on Mars

Curiosity Rover
exploring Mars

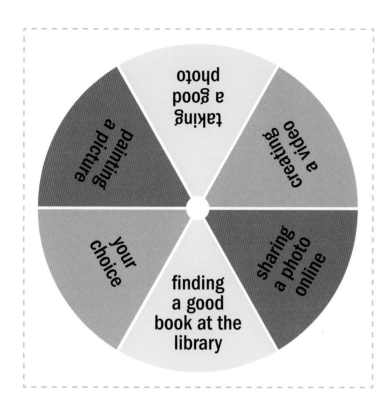

'Can you tell a visual story?'

'Ami Vitale tells stories with her photos.'

'Use quality pencils and pens for drawing.'

'Stop reading so many comic books.'

'I prefer realistic art to abstract art.'

'Videos are one way to tell a story.'

'I will learn to create animations.'

'Do you like manga?'

'Illustrators change their work many times before publishing it.'

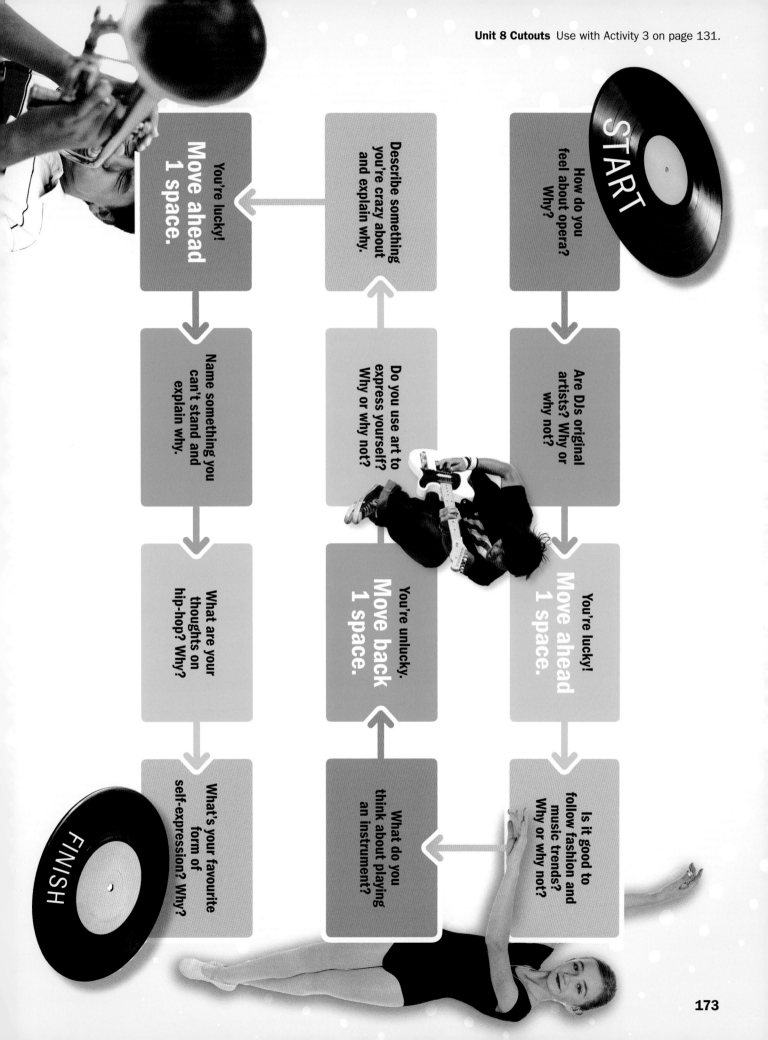

START

How do you feel about opera? Why?

Are DJs original artists? Why or why not?

You're lucky! Move ahead 1 space.

Is it good to follow fashion and music trends? Why or why not?

What do you think about playing an instrument?

Describe something you're crazy about and explain why.

You're lucky! Move ahead 1 space.

Name something you can't stand and explain why.

Do you use art to express yourself? Why or why not?

You're unlucky. Move back 1 space.

What are your thoughts on hip-hop? Why?

What's your favourite form of self-expression? Why?

FINISH

173

Hear an
orchestra play

See a puppeteer
perform

Watch a DJ spin

See an opera
singer perform

Watch a
clown juggle

Hear actors talk

Your choice!
Use see, *feel,*
hear or *watch.*

Feel your
heart beat loudly

Your choice!
Use see, *feel,*
hear or *watch.*

Feel the
floor move

See dancers
perform

Your choice!
Use see, *feel,*
hear or *watch.*